WALKING
WITH THE
LORD

CONTRIBUTING WRITERS:

Christine A. Dallman

Marie D. Jones

Publications International, Ltd.

Louis Weber, CEO
Publications International, Ltd.
7373 North Cicero Avenue
Lincolnwood, Illinois 60712

Permission is never granted for commercial purposes.

ISBN-13: 978-1-60553-973-7
ISBN-10: 1-60553-973-2

Manufactured in China.

8 7 6 5 4 3 2 1

Library of Congress Control Number: 2010923317

CONTENTS

A JOURNEY WITH GOD

❊ ❊ ❊

The idea of walking along a path is a wonderful biblical metaphor for our life experience. We readily relate to the psalmist's description of the Good Shepherd leading us to green pastures and beside still waters, guiding us in paths of righteousness. But then there is that dark valley where the shadow of death lingers and where our doubts may rise up and our fears may threaten our faith. We hesitate there, and sometimes we falter. We may wonder, *How could the psalmist declare at such times, "I will fear no evil"?*

This book poignantly probes that aspect of our life's journey. In a spirit of perplexed wonder, it seeks to understand the parts of the path that don't make sense and that seem as if God has forgotten to be good and faithful as he promised to be. From this book's perspective, it was at the most difficult times that God seemed to have abandoned his child.

When your life has been at its darkest, and your journey has been most frustrating and painful, have you ever wondered or even shouted in anger, "God, where *are* you?!"

It is a question for the ages. It is a question that points to our deepest longings. It holds our greatest fear, our most profound need, and even our highest hope. It is the question that begs for the assurance that the psalmist gave when he said confidently, "I will fear no evil." Why didn't he fear? Why in that valley of the shadow of death did he feel safe and sure? The reason he gives is summed up in five profound words of faith: "For you are with me." He believed that, even in the worst times, God really *was* there.

Walking with the Lord is a stepping stone to developing a deeper trust in God's abiding presence. Right now the bumps in the road may still trip us up, the disappointments may sometimes make us stumble, and our pain may cause us to question God's goodness and love. But as we continue on the journey, seeking to walk with God, our faith is sure to become stronger each day of our lives.

In fact, the day-to-day nature of life's journey *is* the subject of this prayer book. It helps you by providing encouragement for your daily walk. It also reminds you that God is with you, is for you, and loves you, no matter what your circumstance is and no matter what your fears or doubts, questions or concerns are.

Prayers contained in *Walking with the Lord* are written as honest, heartfelt dialogue with God. In fact, you're likely to hear the echoes of your own struggles in them, as well as encouragement that will foster your growing faith in God's love for you. As you make your way through these pages, it is our prayer that you will find yourself declaring with renewed faith, "I will fear no evil, Lord, for I *know* you are with me."

CHAPTER 1

THOUGH UNSEEN, THE LORD IS PRESENT

✖ ✖ ✖

Dear Lord, I sometimes feel as if you don't hear me, or see me, or care about me. I feel lost even when I call out to you, for it seems as though you do not answer me. I pray for the discernment of your Holy Spirit. I know you are always there, but when my faith wavers, I find myself looking to outside things for proof, and yet I know that the proof of you exists in my heart. Please help me remember that yours is a quiet presence that does not shout or attract attention or use big gestures to make yourself known. Help me remember that you are always at my side and that what my eyes cannot see, my heart truly can. Amen.

✳ ✳ ✳

Holy God, your constant and ever-present love is my strength and my foundation. When all around me falls to pieces, I know that with your Spirit to guide me, I can put those pieces back together and be stronger than ever before. You are the wind that allows me to soar and the breath that gives me life. Though I never see your face, I see your countenance upon the smiles of my friends, in the laughter of my children, and throughout the challenges and miracles that occur each day. I need nothing else than to know that you never leave me and that you live within my heart, my soul, and my spirit. Thank you, God.

❊ ❊ ❊

*"Beneath the touch of a helping hand, we can
feel God's strong grasp. If we hold on,
we are no longer alone."*

❊ ❊ ❊

Heavenly Father, reach out to me
today with the touch of your presence.
I am anxious about many things that
I will have to face this day. I long to
know that I am not alone and that you
will be right here with me to guide me
to the right actions and decisions that
are the highest and best for all concerned. Let me feel the soft push of
your loving hands as you gently direct
my steps, and I will open my heart to
listen to the whispers of wisdom you
have for me and for my situation

today. Touch my spirit with yours, and
lead me to better days ahead. Amen.

※ ※ ※

*I sought the Lord, and he answered me, and
delivered me from all my fears. Look to him, and be
radiant; so your faces shall never be ashamed. This
poor soul cried, and was heard by the Lord.*

—Psalm 34:4–6

✳ ✳ ✳

Almighty God, your love is like a pair of invisible arms that hold me up when I am about to fall and lift me up when I am down. My faith assures me that your presence is the eternal grace that I can always count on to carry me when my own strength is simply not enough. I may not see you standing there behind me, but my heart hears your voice telling me I am never alone. Your love is like a pair of invisible wings upon which I can soar above the challenges and problems of the day.

❋ ❋ ❋

My Lord and Savior, are you here for me today? I can't feel your presence, and my lack of faith and trust is getting the better of me right now. Please help me move beyond fear and doubt and know that you are always here and always ready to be my rock and my foundation. My human qualities sometimes keep me from being reminded of my constant connection to you, and I ask that you remind me once again of that connection, as I rise to face the day. Thank you, Lord.

❋ ❋ ❋

Our hope is built on our Lord's faithfulness. He's there with you now. Trust Him.

—Lloyd John Ogilvie

❈ ❈ ❈

Holy God, are you here with me? It's me again, asking for your direction and guidance. Bless me with your mercy and grace that I may do the right thing and say the right thing in every situation I encounter. With you as my constant companion, my everlasting Father, I know that my words and deeds shall be your will and not mine, for my will is often not the best choice. I ask for your wise council today and every day and that you forever remain at my side. Thanks be to you, God.

❈ ❈ ❈

⚜ ⚜ ⚜

Every valley shall be lifted up, and every mountain and hill be made low; the uneven ground shall become level, and the rough places a plain. Then the glory of the Lord shall be revealed, and all people shall see it together, for the mouth of the Lord has spoken.

—Isaiah 40:4–5

⚜ ⚜ ⚜

Heavenly Father, here I am before you, asking for your loving care. My faith in you is what gets me through the trying times in life, and your constant presence keeps the flame of hope alive in my heart when the darkness threatens to surround me. Shower me with your mercy, that I may be made stronger and more resilient in the wake of your love and attention. So please take my hands and pull me up and onto my feet, ready to walk the path you have set out before me. I have faith in you, Holy Father, now and forever. In Jesus' name, I pray. Amen.

❊ ❊ ❊

Dear God, I don't thank you often enough for the miracles you work in my life each and every day. They may not always be big spectacular miracles, but even the smallest reminders of your presence serve to make my heart sing and my spirit soar. Thank you for always being here, no matter how badly I screw up or what dumb mistakes I make in the course of my life. You never judge nor condemn, and you are quick to forgive and show mercy. Thank you for being the loving God that you are, even when it takes every ounce of my faith to believe that you are here with me.

❋ ❋ ❋

"When the world around us grows cold and chaotic, faith is the balm that soothes a fearful heart and the blanket that comforts an anxious mind."

❈❈ ❈❈ ❈❈

O Lord, why do I always have to see
something to believe in it? I know that
you are not something I can see, hear,
or touch, and yet you are in everything
I see, everything I hear, and everything
I touch. Your Spirit confirms for me
the power of faith—of believing in
what cannot be seen. Your power in
my life to heal and forgive confirms for
me that you deeply love me and reveal
your love in the people who care for
me, in the wonder of nature, in the
laughter of a young child, and in the
grateful sounds of my pet. Your presence permeates my life, dear Lord,
even if I cannot look into your eyes.
I am truly blessed with your presence
in my life.

※ ※ ※

*The Lord, your God, is in your midst, a warrior
who gives victory; he will rejoice over you with
gladness, he will renew you in his love;
he will exult over you with loud singing.*

—ZEPHANIAH 3:17

※ ※ ※

Almighty God, I sometimes feel abandoned and alone, as if you have left me and forgotten me. But then something happens, some small miracle or mercy that reminds me that I am never forgotten. Maybe my life continues to be challenging, but I can feel you holding my hand and carrying me when I am faltering under the weight of my fear and doubt. Your footprints in the sand of my life serve to remind me that no matter how dark the night, no matter how difficult the days, you are here ready to take my burdens and carry me to better days ahead.

❈ ❈ ❈

"When we cry out for the blessing of mercy, God hears us."

❈ ❈ ❈

Father in heaven, it's a new day and a new opportunity for me to do your loving work in the world. So please, Lord God, let me be a mirror of your love and compassion to others. You never fail me, even when I am low on faith and trust. You never leave me, even when I look around my life and feel that you have abandoned me. I know that you are always here for me, and I want to go and be there for others and be an unseen and invisible force for love for good—that is, for you. Amen.

❈ ❈ ❈

For truly I tell you, if you have faith the size of a mustard seed, you will say to this mountain, "Move from here to there," and it will move; and nothing will be impossible for you.

—Matthew 17:20

❈ ❈ ❈

In you, dear God, I place my faith. In your presence I find the courage I need to face any challenge and the fortitude I need to overcome any obstacle. Your unseen presence is the force of love in my life that keeps me on the path you have set out before me, unwavering in

my devotion to you and the divine
plan you have ordained for me.
Though you cannot be seen with
physical eyes, I see you in every blessing of my life, as well as the tougher
times that make me stronger and more
resilient. I place my faith in you, and
I pray in the name of your most precious Son, Jesus. Amen.

❊ ❊ ❊

When you close your doors, and make darkness
within, remember never to say that you are alone,
for you are not alone; nay, God is within.

—EPICTETUS

❊ ❊ ❊

My God, I am not always good at
believing in what my eyes cannot see
and what my senses cannot discern,
but I know that you are everywhere in
my life. I look around at all the blessings I have, and my heart is filled with
gratitude for the gifts you have chosen
to give me. I look around at the trials
you have asked me to undertake, and I
realize that you are my teacher as well
as my friend. I do not have to see you
to believe in you, just as you have

always believed in me. Thank you,
God, for opening the eyes of my heart.

✵ ✵ ✵

*For once you were darkness, but now in the Lord
you are light. Live as children of light—for the
fruit of the light is found in all that is
good and right and true.*

—Ephesians 5:8–9

✵ ✵ ✵

Dear Lord, the storms of my life often
threaten to blow me away, and I feel
small and weak and insignificant. Let
me hear that still, small voice within
that reminds me you are always with
me, keeping me safe even as the cold
winds blow and even as the hard rains
fall. Let me feel the warmth of your
ever-present love when life chills me to

the bone and while I seek comfort in
the shelter of a safe harbor.

※ ※ ※

My supreme Lord, your love alone is
all I need to get through each day and
night, and your grace is my salvation.
I need not focus on the things happening outside of me, but on the strength
inside me that is your presence. You
are my light; like the beacon of a
lighthouse you lead me to safe shores.
You are my sun that warms the ice I
stumble upon, making my path easier
to travel. You fill my heart with your
mercy, dear God, and I thank you for
your presence in my life.

※ ※ ※

"Storms sometimes arrive in our lives with hurricane-force winds. We feel as if our hearts are caught in the vortex. But just when we think we'll be destroyed, a still, small voice appears in the eye of the storm to remind us that we are not alone."

❈ ❈ ❈

O God, whom or what shall I fear when you walk beside me? Nothing can disturb the inner peace that comes from knowing that I'm not alone. No matter how lonely I may feel on the outside, I have a friend, a confidante, a cheerleader, a supporter, and, most of all, a loving Father. You are always here for me, and all I have to do is pray to you, for you are all those things to me. You have never failed me, God,

and I hope that I can be more perfect
in your eyes as I follow your guidance
and live your loving will in my life.
Why should I be afraid? I have you,
God, as my partner. Thank you.

⁂ ⁂ ⁂

*The wind blows where it chooses, and you hear the
sound of it, but you do not know where it comes
from or where it goes. So it is with everyone
who is born of the Spirit.*

—JOHN 3:8

※ ※ ※

Dear God, my body feels tired and
weak today. I'm not feeling well, and
I need to know that you are here with
me, making me stronger just by your
presence alone. Knowing that you will
never give me more than I can handle
helps me understand that there is a
reason for what I'm going through, and
it makes the challenges somewhat
easier. Your will may be mysterious,
but I know that your love is real. I rely
on you, God, for my physical strength
and my spiritual strength as well.
Thank you, God.

※ ※ ※

O Lord, reach out to me and give me
your silent strength today. I'm unable

to do this on my own, and I know that
with you supporting me, nothing will
be impossible to overcome. You are my
rock and my cornerstone. You are the
guiding force in my life that moves
through my heart and my soul like a
gentle and comforting breeze. Reach
out to me today and let me know that
I can, and that I will, persevere with
your help. Thank you, Lord, for always
caring for me and for never abandoning me. Amen.

❋ ❋ ❋

I can rely on Him alone—for physical
strength as for every other need.

—CATHERINE MARSHALL

✵ ✵ ✵

My Lord, come walk with me today.
I need a friend, and you have never
forsaken me. Come speak in your still,
sweet voice so that my soul may find
answers to the questions that I alone
cannot find. Come stay with me
through each challenge, and celebrate
with me the blessings that greet me
along the way. My faith in you is
strong, and my belief in your love
unwavering. Come walk with me
today, Lord, as you have walked with
me each day before this.

※ ※ ※

Therefore I tell you, do not worry about your life,
what you will eat, or about your body,
what you will wear. For life is more than food,
and the body more than clothing.

—LUKE 12:22–23

※ ※ ※

God, you have always been faithful
and true. You have never failed to be
here for me, and you have never failed
to help me learn the lessons brought
by both my struggles and blessings. I
place my entire trust in you, knowing
that you will never lead me astray and
never abandon me even when others
in my life consider me down for the
count. Yes, you have blessed me with
wonderful friends and family, but I

place my faith in you alone, for your power and your presence transcend all things seen and all things unseen. You are a mighty and wonderful God, and my faith is my gift to you.

❈ ❈ ❈

Dear Lord, the flame of hope within my heart is dying, and I ask for you to renew my faith and restore my strength. I know that you are here, watching over me, but right now I need a little extra guidance and encouragement. Like a child who needs her blanket, I ask to be wrapped in your loving care so that the flame of hope is rekindled and burns bright within me again. Renew me, Lord; renew my hope and my faith. Amen.

❈ ❈ ❈

*"Even in the face of struggles and difficulties,
there is a higher order of goodness at work in our
lives. We may not be able to physically detect it
at all times, but our faith knows the truth,
and the truth sets us free."*

❈ ❈ ❈

Let the truth of your loving presence
set me free, dear God, of the fears and
worries of this day. Let the truth of
your divine mercy set me free from
the doubts and anxieties I feel as I
meet each new challenge. Let the truth
of your forgiveness be the soothing
balm that restores my relationships
with those I love. You alone are the
truth, dear God. You are the higher
force in my life, bringing order to the

chaos of my spirit. Let the truth set me free, dear God.

※ ※ ※

Blessed are you who are poor, for yours is the Kingdom of God. Blessed are you who are hungry now, for you will be filled. Blessed are you who weep now, for you will laugh.

—Luke 6:20–21

※ ※ ※

Father in heaven, how can I sleep with this worry and fear keeping me awake all night? Bring me the peace only you can provide—the peace that passes all understanding and calms the stormy seas in my soul. I have done all I can do today, and I ask that you help me with those things I cannot control. Your presence, although unseen, is a

constant in my life, and right now, I
need that constant presence to remind
me that even as I lay my head to rest,
you remain awake and alert, watching
over me, protecting me, and loving me.

※ ※ ※

Have courage for the great sorrows of life and
patience for the small ones; and when you have
laboriously accomplished your daily task,
go to sleep in peace. God is awake.

—Victor Hugo

❈ ❈ ❈

What is grace, God? It is the love I feel
when I know you are with me, walking
beside me and offering me guidance
and wisdom. What is faith, God? It is
my belief in you, even if I cannot hold
your hand or see your face. What is
hope, God? It is the joy within my
heart when I realize that I can overcome any challenge as long as you are
with me. What is love, God? It is you
and the blessings you give me.

❈ ❈ ❈

*The one who comes from above is above all; the one
who is of earth belongs to the earth and
speaks about earthly things. The one who
comes from heaven is above all.*

—JOHN 3:31

※ ※ ※

There but for the grace of you, God, go I. Protected by this unseen force that is made up of your love for me and my faith in you. Comforted by this unseen warmth that envelops me and keeps me from suffering through the coldest nights. Guided by this unseen whisper that tells me where to go, what to say, and what to do when my own mind is in too much turmoil to think and my heart is too hurt to feel. There but for the grace of you, God, go I. I am blessed. I am loved. I am grateful. Thank you, God. I pray in Jesus' precious name. Amen.

※ ※ ※

CHAPTER 2

THE LORD WALKS BESIDE ME

❊ ❊ ❊

O heavenly Father, even on a short
journey it's one thing to have a map
and an entirely different thing—a far
better and more assuring thing—to
have a guide. Thank you for being my
guide in this lifelong journey, for taking up the road with me and giving
me the benefit of your wisdom and
the pleasure of your company along
the way. I would be lost and lonely
without you, but because you walk
with me, I am confident and content.

❊ ❊ ❊

When I met Christ at the crossroads of life,
he showed me which way to go
by walking it with me.

—Anonymous

※ ※ ※

Along this path of life, Lord Jesus, I've
come to realize that no person can be
to me what you are. There is a wide
spectrum of disappointment I have
experienced at the hands of others
(including disappointments with
myself). Some letdowns have been
inadvertent and easy to forgive. Others
have been intentional and mean-
spirited, and I have struggled to leave
these deeper hurts in your hands. But
with you, Lord, there is perfect love
and support, pure mercy and forgiveness. You are my source of unfailing
companionship, and I'm deeply grateful that you walk beside me.

※ ※ ※

❈ ❈ ❈

With the Lord on my side I do not fear. What can mortals do to me? The Lord is on my side to help me....It is better to take refuge in the Lord than to put confidence in mortals.

—PSALM 118:6–8

❈ ❈ ❈

Lord Jesus, sometimes I feel as if you can't possibly see my circumstances, because I have difficulty believing it would be your will for me to go through such dark times, times during which I feel isolated, defeated, and without recourse. But then I hear your still, small voice reminding me that I'm not alone, that you are in control, and that your will does not center in circumstances. Rather, your will is rooted in your perfect love for me, and its purpose is to develop the kind of character I need to enjoy a meaningful life and have a deep fellowship with you. Thank you for drawing near to me and encouraging me today.

※ ※ ※

There are times when all of us feel comfortless and helpless, but there is great strength in remembering the one who abides with us.

—"Victories in the Valleys of Life"

❈ ❈ ❈

When I woke up this morning, Lord, my mind filled up with all the unfinished business of my life—indeed, with an accompanying emotional stew of anxiety, panic, dread, and shame. So often the stuff of life seems like too much to handle. But then I turn to you, and I find you are right here with me. You are my reprieve, Lord; you are the best part of everything in my world. I call on you, and you calm me. I look to you, and you show me a peaceful way through the chaos. I remember you, and I find a place of rejoicing. Then I realize again that my life in this world is only for a time, but your presence is my eternal reward.

※ ※ ※

Nevertheless I am continually with you; you hold my right hand. You guide me with your counsel, and afterward you will receive me with honor. Whom have I in heaven but you? And there is nothing on earth that I desire other than you.

—Psalm 73:23–25

※ ※ ※

Thank you, my supreme Lord, for the gift of prayer—the gift of being able to talk with you and the ability to sense your listening and responding through your Spirit and your Word. Thank you, too, for the people you've placed in my life who express your love to me in practical, tangible ways. By these gifts from your hand, I experience comfort both within and without. By

these precious provisions, I know you
love me and walk beside me.

❈ ❈ ❈

"Exhausted from walking this troubling road, we
encounter those who care; truly they are only a
phone call away. Because they are near and
knowing that God is as close as a prayerful
thought, we feel care spread like wings over
us, and we can finally sleep."

❊ ❊ ❊

Your nearness, dear Lord, is a fact not
based on my feelings nor on my circumstances. It is a powerful reality—
a goodness that is strong and constant,
a place of refuge and stability in this
crazy, ever-changing world. I see others struggling without you sometimes,
and I just want to tell them that you
are here for them. I want to tell them
that you have been my source of
strength, courage, help, support, and
comfort—in fact, everything I need!
Please give me the right words to
convey—in ways that people can
perceive and consider—the reality of
your nearness, as well as the blessing
of your presence.

❈ ❈ ❈

For me it is good to be near God; I have made the Lord God my refuge, to tell of all your works.

—PSALM 73:28

❈ ❈ ❈

Dear Jesus, the prophet Isaiah was inspired to call you "Wonderful Counselor." If I paid all of my income to the best human counselor, I would probably be helped on some level, but your love, your Spirit, and your Word have more power to transform my heart and mind than any therapist on the face of the earth. Each day as I walk along with you, I hear you speaking words of wisdom, direction, healing, and insight to me. You're not just any counselor; you are the Wonderful Counselor, and I'm honored and

humbled to have you walking beside
me today.

※ ※ ※

"Hold my hand, Lord, so I will not be afraid."

※ ※ ※

Lord Jesus, when I think about "the
valley of the shadow of death," I see
how it can apply, not only to literal
dying but also to life in this world.
Compared to heaven, this is a dark valley where shades of sin and death loom
and linger. But even in the darkness,
I'm filled with faith, hope, and love
because you are with me. Your imple-
ments of encouragement, guidance,
and correction—that is, your Word,
your Spirit, and your people—are

ever-present reminders that you are leading me safely through the dangers and difficulties of this world.

❈ ❈ ❈

Even though I walk through the darkest valley, I fear no evil; for you are with me; your rod and your staff—they comfort me.

—Psalm 23:4

❈ ❈ ❈

Father in heaven, thank you for the fellowship I enjoy with my friends here on earth. I love going for walks with them; we talk and laugh and enjoy the beauty around us. But you know, Father, my favorite walks are the ones I take just with you. You point out beauty and wildlife I likely would have missed had I been chatting with someone else. You give me encouragement, talk me through my troubling situations, and remind me of how much you love me. I come away from our walks thoroughly refreshed, filled with new hope and joy. Thank you for these special moments and for being beside me at all times.

❋ ❋ ❋

I know that your friend and disciple, the Apostle Peter, once stepped out on a stormy sea in faith, Lord Jesus. As he kept his eyes on you, he walked atop the waves. It wasn't until his focus shifted to the terrors of the raging elements around him that he began to be overcome by them. Today, you know what tumultuous situations are ahead of me. Whether big or small, Lord, help me remember to keep my eyes on you and to be more focused on your presence with me than the circumstances around me. Thank you that, in this sense, walking on water is possible for me, too!

❋ ❋ ❋

❋ ❋ ❋

When you pass through the waters, I will be with you; and through the rivers, they shall not overwhelm you; when you walk through fire you shall not be burned, and the flame shall not consume you.

—ISAIAH 43:2

❋ ❋ ❋

I just want to thank you today, Lord Jesus, that though the love of other people may come and go, your love is perfect, persistent, and faithful. I know this because you reveal it to me every day as you walk beside me, protecting me, providing for me, encouraging me, teaching me, and leading me along the path of life. In your love, I am satisfied.

※ ※ ※

Have no fear for what tomorrow may bring. The same loving God who cares for you today will take care of you tomorrow and every day. God will either shield you from suffering or give you unfailing strength to bear it. Be at peace then, and put aside all anxious thoughts and imaginations.

—St. Francis de Sales

※ ※ ※

Help me walk willingly beside you, almighty God, even when, in my estimation, you're doing things all wrong. I know that sounds strange when I say it out loud, but I admit that when I dig my heels in or grumble or accuse you of not caring, I'm really doubting your wisdom and ability to lead me where I need to go. So, Lord,

please help me remember that you
know things I don't, that you see
clearly from the beginning to the end,
and that you love me more deeply
than I can ever fully perceive. In light
of these realities, I will choose to
follow you today without fretting.

Our only task is to keep in step with him. He
chooses the direction and leads the way. As we
walk step by step with him, we soon discover that
we have lost the crushing burden of needing to
take care of ourselves and get our own way, and
we discover that the burden is indeed light.
We come into the joyful, simple life
of hearing and obeying.

—RICHARD FOSTER, *FREEDOM OF SIMPLICITY*

❋ ❋ ❋

Lord Jesus, it's awesome to realize that all authority belongs to you! I want to remember that, because when it feels as if my day, or my life, or the world is spinning out of control, I can be assured that it really isn't. And when it's hard for me to believe or understand this reality, there's the comforting truth that you are walking with me. Thank you for your promise to be with us who belong to you until you bring this world to a conclusion and settle us in our heavenly home.

※ ※ ※

Jesus came and said to them, "All authority in heaven and on earth has been given to me....And remember, I am with you always, to the end of the age."

—Matthew 28:18, 20

※ ※ ※

One of the ways I hear you speak to me along the path of life, Lord Jesus, is through your Word. Sometimes you remind me of a Scripture that was read during a worship service, or a passage I reviewed during a quiet time with you, or maybe a verse I memorized as a child. I find that your Word is a great source of comfort and strength along my path, and the more of it I take in and think about, the

more I understand your deep affection
for me. Thank you for the way you
open up your Word to me. Amen.

❋ ❋ ❋

Jesus, my redeemer, you are the one
who takes my brokenness and gives me
wholeness in return. You are the one
who takes my mistakes and turns
them into blessings. You are the one
who forgives my sins and fills me with
your own righteousness so that I can
be in fellowship with you. How can I
praise and thank you enough for coming alongside me and transforming my
troubled heart into a rejoicing one?
I can begin today by taking my place
beside you—the place you have made
for me by your redemptive love.

❊ ❊ ❊

No matter what deep hurt you have experienced,
He is able to redeem it. If you allow Jesus to walk
with you.... He will take your valley of trouble
and give you a Door of Hope.

—JAN FRANK

❊ ❊ ❊

How grateful I am today for your Holy
Spirit, Lord Jesus! He reveals himself
to me as my comforter—the one who
teaches me, leads me into all truth,
and ministers as my intercessor. No
wonder that, even though I cannot see
you, Jesus, I can sense your nearness to
me. By your Spirit, you walk beside me
every step of the way. I praise you for
the gift of your presence through the
ministry of the Holy Spirit.

※ ※ ※

[Jesus said to his followers,] "I will ask the Father, and he will give you another Advocate, to be with you forever. This is the Spirit of truth. . . . You know him, because he abides with you, and he will be in you."

—John 14:16–17

※ ※ ※

Lord God, your Word tells me to keep in step with your Spirit so that I won't gratify the impulses of my human nature that are harmful and destructive to my soul. I admit that sometimes I wade around in my swamp of selfishness when I could be walking lightly and heartily in fellowship with you. I need your forgiveness today for the ways I've ignored you and turned to my own devices. I truly want to walk beside you in the warmth and light of your presence and the peace of your ways. I'm ready to begin again. Help me keep in step with you today and every day. In Jesus' precious name, I pray. Amen.

❈❈ ❈❈ ❈❈

Heavenly Father, I remember some
of the epic experiences of my life.
Highlights and "lowlights" parade
through my memory, but as they do,
I realize that they often lose their
power over time. The days and weeks
and months smooth the novelty,
excitement, pain, and pleasure until
I'm engulfed again by "everydayness."
I live, and life continually changes me,
but one thing remains the same: the
fact that you are with me. Nothing
changes that—not mountains, not
valleys, nor the days that wear them
into plains. Thank you, dear Father,
for always being you and for always
loving me.

※ ※ ※

"How comforting to know that God tends to us
as we move through life's extremes! He is here
with us in births and deaths and in stillness and
activity. We find the courage to live through these
present moments and to move into the future,
knowing that we cannot wander so far in any
direction that he is not already there."

※ ※ ※

You have often called to me in different ways, Lord, inviting me to walk
with you and to experience the blessing of your nearness. Thank you for
your kind intentions toward me. I
realize now that even when it has
taken hardship and struggle to get my
attention, your desire has always been
to bless me. I'm truly glad you have

directed me away from destructive choices and paths and have led me into paths that bring life and peace. I owe you everything, and yet you do not take anything from me that I do not choose to give freely. May I always choose to seek you, Lord, to desire your nearness, and to know the blessings of walking beside you.

✳ ✳ ✳

Incline your ear, and come to me; listen, so that you may live.... Seek the Lord while he may be found, call upon him while he is near.

—ISAIAH 55:3, 6

❋ ❋ ❋

It's good to know, Lord, that whether I speak these prayers aloud or lift them up in silence from the depths of my heart, you hear, you listen, and you respond. I know that sometimes I've complained that you're not answering my prayers. I'm sorry for those times of faithless frustration. I know that you always answer but often not in the timing or the way I expect. I'm glad, though, that you're not bound to my expectations. I've seen you bring wonderful answers to my needs and dilemmas that I never could have dreamed up. Your creativity and perfect wisdom never stop astounding me. I will keep praying to you as long as I live because I know you walk with me.

❋ ❋ ❋

You need not cry very loud: he is nearer
to us than we think.

—Brother Lawrence

❋ ❋ ❋

O Lord, help me not run ahead
today—that is, ahead of your direction
and guidance. Help me not lag behind,
either, Lord—that is, behind your call
to love and forgive and do what is
right. Help me remain in the place
to which you call me—that place
reserved for me beside you. May I be
tethered to your side by my willing
hand held in your gentle one. I don't
want to miss out on one moment of
fellowship with you today.

❈ ❈ ❈

I would rather walk with God in the dark
than go alone in the light.

—Mary Gardiner Brainard

❈ ❈ ❈

Walking with you is like an unlimited
benefits package, Lord! Without any
premium to pay, I have your promise
to deliver, protect, answer, be with,
rescue, and honor me. Oh, and you
have thrown in a long life and salvation on top of it all. Who is as blessed
as I am? Only those who also know
your love and the wonderful benefits
of walking in it. Lord Jesus, help each
of us hold fast to you as we point
others toward you as well.

CHAPTER 3

THE LORD ALWAYS HELPS ME

❈ ❈ ❈

Almighty God, I need your help more than ever. I can't seem to find the answers to the problems that keep plaguing my life. I have tried to use my will to make everything right, but I finally realize that I must now surrender my will to yours and let you do your miracles. And so I give my burdens to you, trusting that you will smooth out all the rough edges and calm all the stormy seas in my life. Thank you, God, for your help in my times of need. Amen.

❈ ❈ ❈

"Turn your problems over to God, and he will orchestrate the best outcome."

※ ※ ※

Dear Lord, when the last flicker of
hope seems to go out in my heart and
my spirit is ready to give up, you come
to me and show me more mercy
and more grace, and I'm renewed in
strength. I know that you will never
give me more trouble than I can handle and that in those times when I
don't believe I can handle more, you
will come to me and carry me through
the darkest valleys. For this, Lord, I'm
forever grateful.

※ ※ ※

*Blessed are those who trust in the Lord, whose trust
is the Lord. They shall be like a tree planted by
water, sending out its roots by the stream.*

—Jeremiah 17:7–8

❧ ❧ ❧

Holy God, things are tough lately, and I could use a helping hand from above to get through it all. Show me how to make the right choices and do the right things to make life more joyful. I ask you today in prayer to stand beside me and be my column of strength when I need something strong to lean upon. My faith in you tells me I can always lean on you, God, no matter how bad things seem to me, for I know that you are here ready to intervene on my behalf. Amen.

❈ ❈ ❈

*"No matter how deep a rut we dig ourselves into,
the arms of God are long enough to lift us up to
a newer life, free from struggle. No matter how
dark a tunnel we crawl into, the love of God is
strong enough to reach in and guide us toward
a brighter life, free from fear."*

❈ ❈ ❈

Today, dear Lord, I ask for your mercy
and compassion. Today, I ask for your
divine love and wisdom. Today, I ask
for your guidance and your strength.
I ask that you do for me what is out
of my control to do and that you show
me the way that my own human eyes
fail to see: the way to happiness, joy,
and love. I surrender to your loving
will for my life, for I know that my

mind cannot always grasp the bigger picture you have in store for me. Today, Lord, I ask for your help in keeping me on the path you have made for me and me alone. Thank you, Lord.

❋ ❋ ❋

My Lord, I pray to you today from the depths of my heart. I feel as if I can't deal with so much of what is happening around me, and I ask that you help share these burdens with me. With your grace and power, I will be able to conquer what I alone can't conquer and what I alone can't understand. Your gentle helping hand can provide me with the divine guidance I seek, when my own mind can't find the way and when my spirit is unsure. I pray to you, dear Lord, to come to my aid today. Amen.

※ ※ ※

You, O Lord, are a shield around me, my glory, and the one who lifts up my head. I cry aloud to the Lord, and he answers me from his holy hill. I lie down and sleep; I wake again, for the Lord sustains me.

—Psalm 3:3–5

※ ※ ※

Great God in heaven, I'm broken and tired, and I don't think I can carry on much longer without help from you. I've tried all I can to make things work, and still I feel miserable and stuck. I pray that today you will work your mysterious ways in my life and show me open doors that I can't see

with my own eyes. Please direct me
to solutions that my mind simply
can't think of right now. I pray for
the miracle of your presence, while
bringing a new perspective to my eyes,
a new hope to my heart, and a new
strength to my spirit. Amen.

❋ ❋ ❋

Dear God, I'm filled with gratitude for
the awesome ways you always seem to
be here for me when I need you most.
Either with an inspiration that comes
to me from out of nowhere, or a call
from a friend when I feel utterly alone,
or some wonderful new opportunity
that appears when I'm about to give
up, you are my miracle worker. I'm
truly thankful for the good things you

bless me with, as well as the challenges
that make me stronger and more
resilient. I know that whatever you
send my way is for my highest good,
and I receive it all with open arms.
Thank you, God.

❈ ❈ ❈

God is in the midst of every situation, and when
you are ready, He will reveal the splendor
of your own life.

—MARY MANIN MORRISSEY

❈ ❈ ❈

Lord God, today is a bright new day,
filled with new ideas and opportuni-
ties. You never fail to come to my aid
by giving me new eyes to see the world
with each morning, no matter how
dark and long the night before might
have been. I awaken, and I feel as
though something has shifted, and I
know that you have somehow come
once again into my heart and refilled it
with love and forgiveness and courage,
just what I needed in order to rise this
morning feeling stronger than ever.
You never fail me, God, and I thank
you for that. I pray I can always make
you proud of me in return. Amen.

❈ ❈ ❈

✳ ✳ ✳

Strengthen the weak hands, and make firm the feeble knees. Say to those who are of a fearful heart, "Be strong, do not fear! Here is your God."

—Isaiah 35:3–4

✳ ✳ ✳

Heavenly Father, I have so many questions that I just can't seem to find the answers for. I feel lost and alone and without direction, as if I'm wandering aimlessly through my own life. I pray that you will help me find the answers I seek and the direction my life should take so that I can live my best life possible. Because you see all the things I cannot and because your perspective is much bigger than mine, I will listen for your guidance and

follow the direction of your loving
will. Amen.

❈ ❈ ❈

My Lord, why does it sometimes seem
as though nothing is going right and
every door available to me is closing in
my face? Help me see that it is you
closing those doors and leaving open
only the right one for me. Help me
have the faith and the patience to wait
for that open door to appear in my life
and not be so anxious that I enter the
wrong door. Help me trust in your
wisdom and surrender to your will,
knowing that soon my door will be
opened before me.

❈ ❈ ❈

"Whenever we are uncertain as to our course, we can rely on God to shut each door against us— every door except the right one."

❈ ❈ ❈

Father God, I need a sign today to show me the way toward happiness and joy. I need a word, an image, or a person to appear that my heart and my spirit will recognize as a sign sent from you. Help me discern your loving guidance in the daily events of my life and hear your gentle encouragement when those events threaten to derail my peace of mind. Send me a sign or two today, and give me the wisdom to understand them when I see them. Thank you, Father.

※ ※ ※

Then Jonah prayed to the Lord his God from the belly of the fish, saying, "I called to the Lord out of my distress, and he answered me; out of the belly of Sheol I cried, and you heard my voice."

—JONAH 2:1–2

※ ※ ※

How could I ever feel alone, dear God, when you have provided me with so many wonderful friends who rarely let me down? I know that these are human angels you have sent into my life to stand beside me through thick and thin. There is no greater blessing than the love of those who care, and you have given me so many people who care and through whom you do your wondrous workings in my life.

※ ※ ※

At the time I need strength, God puts it in my heart or provides it through someone who is close to me. I don't bring it about. It's a gift.

—DAVE DRAVECKY

※ ※ ※

Father God, where are you when I need you? Why, of course, you're right here at my side. I come to you today not to ask for something but to thank you for always being here at the exact moment I need you in the flash of an idea or the certainty of a decision, in the sense of which direction to take or a brilliant inspiration. I know that no matter what is going on in my life, I can always count on you to be with me, telling me exactly what I need to

hear when I need it. Thank you so
much, Father.

※ ※ ※

*Now I am about to go the way of all the earth, and
you know in your hearts and souls, all of you, that
not one thing has failed of all the good things that
the Lord your God promised concerning you;
all have come to pass for you, not one
of them has failed.*

—Joshua 23:14–15

※ ※ ※

Lord, help me understand why the
things that happen in my life sometimes have to be exceedingly difficult.
I'm tired of the struggle, and I'm
exhausted from trying to keep all the
balls I'm juggling in the air. I worry
they will fall to the ground and my

whole life will shatter. Please send me
your merciful grace so I can handle my
life with more courage, strength, and
patience. Your saving grace renews my
spirit and even my physical strength so
I can take on each struggle as it comes.

※ ※ ※

*My thoughts are not your thoughts, nor are your
ways my ways, says the Lord. For as the heavens
are higher than the earth, so are my ways
higher than your ways, and my thoughts
than your thoughts.*

—Isaiah 55:8–9

❋ ❋ ❋

Dear God, I don't need a big bolt of lightning to strike me or a loud voice from the heavens to boom down from above telling me what to do. I know that you speak in much gentler, quieter ways. All I ask today is to be aware of your gentle wisdom when you choose to impart it and that I'm not too busy or stressed out to hear your whispers of guidance when they come. I don't need big shows of your love, God. Small ones will do just fine.

❋ ❋ ❋

It must make you laugh, Lord God, the way I always try to control everything and think I'm in charge. I know that you're in charge and that is best because right now, I have no idea what I'm doing. When I set my human ego aside long enough to feel your presence there beside me, I know that answers are coming and solutions are only an inspiration away. So forgive me for those moments when I think I'm running this ship, and with your love and support, continue to remind me that you and you alone are in charge!

❈ ❈ ❈

"Our lives are filled with many questions that may never be answered, but that's okay if we let God lead and direct us. We may not understand why certain things happen or why we have to go through difficult situations, but the one thing we can know for sure is that God is always in control."

✵ ✵ ✵

Dear God, please hear my prayer. I ask for nothing big today, just a little extra love sent my way. It seems as though times have been so trying for me lately that I'm on edge and my patience is wearing thin. Please send me just a little bit of extra courage so I can get through this time with my head on straight and my sanity intact. I know that I can always count on you to carry me where my own feet fear to tread. So carry me now just for a little while. Please, Lord!

✵ ✵ ✵

Here I am again, heavenly Father. I know that I lean on you a lot, but there are times when even my best and

closest friends can't help me the way
you can. I consider you my best friend
and my constant advisor, and I trust
that once again you will intervene in
my life when I'm not sure what to do
or say. I know that I can surrender and
let your thoughts become mine, and
your wisdom guide my feet exactly
where I need to go. Thank you for
always putting up with me, God.

※　※　※

*Listen carefully to me, . . . Incline your ear, and come
to me; listen, so that you may live.*

—ISAIAH 55:2–3

※　※　※

Dear Lord, I think it is about time you
took over the sinking ship of my life. I
can't seem to steer my life in the right

direction when left to my own wits. You alone know what is best for me and where I need to go to fulfill the blessed destiny you have chosen for me. Please take the steering wheel and move me toward that very destiny. I will cast aside my stubborn and selfish will and let your will be my guide and my north star. Thank you, Lord, for adjusting my course and setting right my sails today.

※ ※ ※

*"Wherever we may find ourselves,
God is at the helm of our lives."*

※ ※ ※

O God, this is a scary time for me, and
I could use your spiritual guidance.
I am facing choices that I don't know
if I'm really prepared to make, and I
know that you can see all of the per-
spectives that I'm blind to in my small
existence. Please help me understand
the bigger picture, so I can make the
wisest decisions possible, decisions
based upon love, compassion, and
empathy. I ask for your guidance in all
my decisions, today and every day,
both the large and the small. Amen.

❈ ❈ ❈

"We are sometimes faced with choices that are scary, risky, and untried, but we can make wise decisions if we rely on God's spiritual guidance."

❈ ❈ ❈

Dear Lord, please lift my spirits higher, because right now they are really low. I try to see the blessings in my challenges, and I know in my heart they are there, but my fears and doubts have a hold on me today. Lift me up out of my troubles and help me see them from a much higher place, where the answers that I never even considered are obvious and the wisdom I have no access to is everywhere. Where you are, Lord, is where my happiness is, so lift my spirits today and help me realize that you have my life in your hands.

❋ ❋ ❋

On wings of angels you carry me, God, when I'm too tired and worn down to walk on my own. Through the valley of darkness you walk ahead, lighting my way so I don't stumble. In the midst of the storm, you calm the seas so that my ship can safely reach the shore up ahead. At the end of a cold night, you bring warmth and comfort to my broken spirit. Thank you, God, for the constant and infinite love you show me, often when I most feel lost, alone, and unloved. That is when I know I will feel those heavenly wings beneath me, carrying me home to you.

❈ ❈ ❈

For God alone my soul waits in silence; from him comes my salvation. He alone is my rock and my salvation, my fortress; I shall never be shaken.

—Psalm 62:1–2

❈ ❈ ❈

I put my trust in you, dear Lord, to show me the rainbow at the end of a long and dreary storm. I believe in you, Lord, because you never fail to give me what I need even before I know I need it. You may not be visible to me, but your presence is always felt in my heart, where your love and mercy are available to me in infinite supply. I may not always turn to you first, Lord, but eventually when I realize I need your divine help, I

always find my way back to the trust
and faith I have in you above all.

※ ※ ※

He's there with you now. Trust Him. And then
expectantly anticipate that at the right time and in
the way that's most creative to you and all
concerned, He will intervene and infuse
you with exactly what you need.
What an exciting way to live!

—Lloyd John Ogilvie

❋❋ ❋❋ ❋❋

Dear Lord, you said that I can always
deliver my burdens to you and that
you will take up my concerns. I try to
handle my own problems as much as
possible, but today I come to you in
prayer because I really need your help.
I will listen for your inspiration and
instruction, and I will do what you
would have me do. I just ask you to
make those instructions clear to me, so
I know the right steps to take. Help me
break through the confusion and fear
and see your active presence in my life.
Thank you, Lord.

❋❋ ❋❋ ❋❋

Almighty God, please take my cares
and my problems and give me a heart

free and at peace again. Because my worrying is getting me nowhere, I'm turning it all over to you so you can do that wonderful work of peace that you do. I know that you don't want me to struggle, and my struggling usually comes from fear, doubt, and resistance. Therefore, today, I'm giving my struggles to you, God, knowing that the perfect outcome is on its way.

❊ ❊ ❊

My child, do not let these escape from your sight; keep sound wisdom and prudence, and they will be life for your soul and adornment for your neck. Then you will walk on your way securely, and your foot will not stumble.

—PROVERBS 3:21–23

※ ※ ※

My Lord and Savior, how much lighter
I feel in heart and in spirit when I cast
my burdens and my cares upon you.
Your strength can do what mine falls
short of. By giving you my concerns,
I'm able to get on with my life with a
more loving spirit and a more kind and
giving heart, just as you would want
me to. Thank you, Lord Jesus, for
always taking from me my heaviest
loads, so I can bring back that spring
to my step and smile to my soul.

※ ※ ※

Let God take care of your problems; cast your care upon Him and do what He has instructed you to do. It almost sounds too good to be true, doesn't it? You can actually enjoy life while God handles all your problems!

—Joyce Meyer

※ ※ ※

It's dark outside, Lord, but like a bright and blazing torch, you are there to light my way and warm my heart. It is cold outside, Lord, but like a tent you are there to shelter me from the storms and comfort me. It is scary out there, Lord, but with you always working on my behalf, , I know that there truly isn't anything to fear at all. For that I'm grateful, Lord. Amen.

CHAPTER 4

GOD IS TRULY FAITHFUL

❊ ❊ ❊

I remember times in the past, Lord, when I did not know whether I could or should rely on you. In my youth there was a sense that I should be able to handle everything on my own, and I felt like a failure when I couldn't. But through the years, my faith has grown, and I now comprehend the truth that calling on you is exactly the right thing to do in all circumstances. My past experiences have taught me to lean fully on you, dear Lord, not worrying about what is ahead today or in the days to come.

❊ ❊ ❊

※ ※ ※

"It helps to look over my shoulder and see the times when God was a ready companion. I feel secure, knowing that he is always waiting to take my hand into tomorrow."

※ ※ ※

Remembering how you have worked in my life, heavenly Father, is what makes me so quick to seek you out for strength and encouragement. I run to you like a little child to a loving parent, whether I'm weeping or rejoicing. I just want to share all of my life with you because I trust your unfailing love for me—a love you have shown to me in so many wonderful ways while I have walked with you. You have never failed to support me. And so I do

rejoice in you as I seek your presence
today! Amen.

※ ※ ※

Let the hearts of those who seek the Lord rejoice. Seek
the Lord and his strength, seek his presence
continually. Remember the wonderful works he has
done, the miracles, and the judgments he uttered.

—1 Chronicles 16:10–12

※ ※ ※

Dear Lord, I'm often nearest to you
when I'm farthest from security in
this life. So often you have used the
uncertainties in my world to help me
become certain of your presence. I
remember, Lord Jesus, the times I had
nowhere else to turn, and you were
there, assuring me and comforting me.
And whenever I've trusted you and

put my burdens in your care, I've
never been more at peace. I long for
that closeness with you today.

❋ ❋ ❋

After proving God's faithfulness for many years,
I can testify that times of want have ever been
times of spiritual blessing, or have led to them.

—A. J. BROOMHALL

❋ ❋ ❋

Somewhere in your Word, God, it says
that perfect love casts out fear. It's
because of you that I know, in at least
one sense, what that passage means.
Over and over, your love has become
evident to me as I've journeyed along
with you through thick and thin. And
because of your track record of unfailing love, my troubles don't keep me

awake anymore. And when I wake up,
if these troubles try to encroach on my
morning, I remember that your love is
with me, and my fears take a backseat
to the faith I have in you.

✵ ✵ ✵

*I remember the days of old, I think about all your
deeds, I meditate on the works of your hands.... Let
me hear of your steadfast love in the morning,
for in you I put my trust.*

—Psalm 143:5, 8

❈ ❈ ❈

It's comforting to have you watching over my life, Father in heaven. Whether I'm awake or asleep, I sense the reality of your presence with me and I'm not afraid. You've taught me that I don't need to fear. Your promise to be with me every day, every hour, and every moment of my life has been upheld and confirmed to me countless times: In my darkest times, I've turned to you, and you've been there; in my most exquisite joys, I've delighted in and with you; and all the times in between, I've talked with you, knowing you hear my prayers. You've continually kept your promise to be with me, and I don't even wonder anymore if you're there. I *know* you are.

❊ ❊ ❊

Things might be muddled and messy right now in some areas of my life, Lord, but today I simply lift these up to you in faith. The path I've walked with you up to now is marked with many monuments of your restoration and redemption. In each of these seemingly impossible situations along my way, you have worked to bring about help, healing, and wholeness. That's why I refuse to stress out about what's amiss today. I will do what I know is right and leave the rest in your capable hands.

❊ ❊ ❊

"As I look back and see God's faithfulness, I'm filled with expectation of all that he

*has in store for me in the future, and
my heart overflows with joy."*

❋ ❋ ❋

One day, heavenly Father, I will look back on my entire life and see it from your perspective. Meanwhile, help me learn the lessons you have given me along the way. Particularly, when painful ordeals come and I cry out in my distress, help me remember to look up. Then help me listen to your comforting Word, which reminds me that you are with me and that you have a plan and purpose for me even in my pain—a plan and purpose that begins in fellowship with you and ends in rejoicing with you in my eternal home.

❈ ❈ ❈

Beloved, do not be surprised at the fiery ordeal that is taking place among you to test you, as though something strange were happening to you. But rejoice insofar as you are sharing Christ's sufferings, so that you may also be glad and shout for joy when his glory is revealed.

—1 PETER 4:12–13

❈ ❈ ❈

If I could control my future, Lord, I'd make a mess of my life for sure. If I could see my future, I would never be able to "be" in the present or benefit from it. So please help me relax and leave the future in your hands. The past holds enough evidence to assure me that you're able to carry me through what lies ahead. Let my faith prevail right now because of your faithfulness up to now.

❆ ❆ ❆

Sometimes, God, the pressures that pile up make me think I'm going to snap like a brittle twig. And just when I think I'm going to be overwhelmed, I call out to you in desperation. It's then that I realize I was trying to make things work through my own strength and according to my own way of thinking. As soon as I turn my face toward you, however, I'm made strong in your strength and strong in the assurance of your help, comfort, and protection. My troubles may be too much for me to handle alone, but as you have shown me time and time

again, they're never too much to handle when my hand is in yours.

❈ ❈ ❈

"I know I can depend on God to see me through
each challenge he allows, because he has always
provided the grace and strength I need to
endure and ultimately triumph."

❈ ❈ ❈

Because faithfulness is part of who you
are, Father in heaven, you will never
be unfaithful to me. What a wonderful
reality! There have been times when I
was tempted to believe you had failed
me, but whenever I've thought that,
I've soon come to realize the truth. I
usually catch myself now before I start
in with any foolish complaints or

accusations aimed at you. It's good to be so thoroughly convinced of how faithful you are, because I know how faithful you've always been. Thank you, Father, that even when I've been unfaithful to you, you have never cast me aside. I pray in the name of your most holy Son, Jesus Christ. Amen.

❋❋ ❋❋ ❋❋

"Some of the greatest lessons we learn are only after our hearts have suffered. For in times of pain, we receive wisdom, and in times of sorrow, we gain understanding."

❋❋ ❋❋ ❋❋

Heavenly Father, I have heard people who have walked with you for decades talk about how good you are to them. Seniors who have spent a lifetime trusting in you are a vast reservoir of testimony about your faithfulness to them. I hear from them how you've seen them through hard times and blessed them in both simple and miraculous ways. Listening to them, dear Father, makes me want to be someone who can easily and readily

talk about how you've seen *me* through
and filled *me* up with good things. My
life is open to you—open to receive
both your care and your faithful guidance all the days of my life.

❈ ❈ ❈

I will proclaim the name of the Lord!…His work is
perfect, and all his ways are just.… Remember the
days of old, consider the years long past; ask your
father, and he will inform you; your elders,
and they will tell you.

—Deuteronomy 32:3–4, 7

❈ ❈ ❈

My Lord, why do bad things happen
to good people? I don't understand
your reasons for allowing so much
suffering in some lives. It appears to
fly in the face of your goodness and

justice and threatens to undermine my faith in your all-knowing, all-powerful, and loving nature. But then I look at Christ: In his life, death, and resurrection, you remind me that there is so much more to life than what meets my eye. Grant me an eternal perspective today, Lord, trusting your wisdom and your final say in all things.

❋ ❋ ❋

Dear Lord, when good things happen
in my life, I often chalk them up to
coincidence, good fortune, my own
savvy, or something else in the
moment they occur. Too often, I fail
to see your kindnesses to me for what
they are: little I-love-you gifts you
send to cheer and encourage me,
reminding me that you see me and are
caring for every detail of my life. Lord,
as I look back on my week and even
further back through months and
years, I see your tender mercies sprin-
kled generously throughout my days.
I just want to say thank you right now
and to tell you that I love you too.

❄ ❄ ❄

"Looking back over the road we've traveled, we sometimes see God more clearly than ever."

❄ ❄ ❄

I know you are looking forward to the day, Lord, when we will be together face to face. So am I! I can't wait for the time when I will look back on my struggles and sufferings like a new mother looks on her labor pains—as something fading quickly into the background of her experience because of her profound joy at having and holding that tiny new life. But I must wait. Help me endure patiently as I anticipate that joyful event.

※ ※ ※

I consider that the sufferings of this present time are not worth comparing with the glory about to be revealed to us.... But if we hope for what we do not see, we wait for it with patience.

—ROMANS 8:18, 25

※ ※ ※

How many sunrises have you granted the world, Lord, up to this day? How many raindrops have fallen on how many harvests? How many meals have sustained how many people throughout the history of humanity? How many hearts have been comforted by your love? What does your faithfulness look like, Lord? Ah, indeed, your faithfulness looks like countless instances of your goodness—so many that we are in danger of taking them for granted. Yet, without these "common" blessings, we begin to suffer and doubt you. We don't wonder why when you give them to us, only when we feel their lack. Perhaps, Lord, reflecting on your goodness is the first step out of my illusion of self-sufficiency. Please strengthen my trust in you today by making me grateful for your faithful ways.

❋ ❋ ❋

"God is dependable, and his never changing nature reminds me that he is in control."

❋ ❋ ❋

How often, dear God, have you sustained my heart with encouragement from your Word? I recall times when I've heard a sermon passage that was just what I needed to hear, or read a calendar with a verse that lifted my spirits, or received a card on which a friend included a Bible quote reminding me of your love, or remembered a Bible verse I learned long ago in a moment of need. Thank you for every instance of blessing in my life that has come to me through your eternal and sacred Word.

※ ※ ※

I bow down toward your holy temple and give thanks to your name for your steadfast love and your faithfulness; for you have exalted your name and your word above everything. On the day I called, you answered me, you increased my strength of soul.

—PSALM 138:2–3

※ ※ ※

Ships are guided to safe harbor by the aid of a lighthouse, airplane pilots have the control tower, and space travelers have mission control. Nevertheless, at times, even these helps have failed in some way. Meanwhile, Lord Jesus, as you guide me safely to my eternal home, you never fail. I never have to wonder if your light will go out, if your communication system will fail, or if you will fall asleep at the switch. I have experienced your strong but gentle guidance, and I know it is infallible. Even when I have been weak and failing, you have been ever faithful. I rest securely in your care.

※ ※ ※

"God is our unshakable foundation. He is our unbending column of strength and hope when all seems lost. In the darkest hour, he is the beacon of light that guides us to the safety of solid ground."

※ ※ ※

O holy God, I most often think about your faithfulness in terms of my physical needs. But where would I be if you hadn't come to minister to my spiritual needs? As I look back and see all that you have provided for my spirit, I rejoice! I see the hope that your promises have brought to my heart; the peace that your presence provides me each day; the balm that your forgiveness is when I confess my sin to you; the comfort that your love gives me when insecurities try to rise up; and the assurance of your strength in me when fear threatens to overwhelm me. My spirit has been brought to life, God, and is kept safe in you!

※ ※ ※

*May the God of peace himself sanctify you entirely;
and may your spirit and soul and body be kept
sound and blameless at the coming of our Lord Jesus
Christ. The one who calls you is faithful,
and he will do this.*

—1 Thessalonians 5:23–24

※ ※ ※

I wish, Lord Jesus, I could help everyone understand how truly wonderful it is to walk with you. If I could write a screenplay of my life, the theme of the story would be your faithfulness. If I could recreate the drama of my direst times, my most difficult struggles, my deepest uncertainties, and my most painful disappointments, I would show how perfectly and precisely you intervened, provided, comforted, and helped; indeed, I feel as if I could convince the world! But I know that each person must make his or her own way to you and then decide whether to receive you or not. But for those who would desire you, Lord, grant me a voice to testify to your faithful love.

※ ※ ※

My future looks bright to me, dear Lord, even when things don't seem to be going my way. But it's not because I have a Pollyanna kind of optimism. No, it's because so many times I've seen you use the most unlikely circumstances—even redeeming my worst blunders—to bring about something surprisingly marvelous. I don't

know how you do it; I just know that
you do. So today I'm watching and
waiting patiently for what you have in
store. Thank you for your excellent
plan for my life.

❈ ❈ ❈

*"In retrospect, we can see how God uses every life
circumstance, disappointment, and joy to reveal
his plan for our good. We can truly trust
in God's faithfulness."*

❈ ❈ ❈

As I have let go of my own goals for
my life to embrace yours, dear Lord,
I have enjoyed great adventure and
great challenge. Meanwhile, my faith
in you has deepened and your peace
has become stronger in my heart. I

have learned to love you more with
each passing year, and I know without
a doubt that you have my good in
mind. What a difference this journey
with you has made in my character!
There is no part of my life that has not
been touched for the better by the
good purposes you have for me.

❈ ❈ ❈

We know that all things work together for good
for those who love God, who are called
according to his purpose.

—ROMANS 8:28

❈ ❈ ❈

I admit, Lord God, there have been
times in the past when I thought you
were tardy in answering my prayers or
remiss in the way you answered them

or ignoring me altogether. That was because I was impatient and had expectations and preconceived notions I was trying to impose on your plan. How foolish I feel when I think about them now! But I'm also encouraged by the way your faithfulness to and patience with me has brought about growth and change in my thinking and behaving. A mature faith is developing as I walk with you. I praise you for this, dear Lord!

CHAPTER 5

GOD'S CHERISHED CHILD

※ ※ ※

Dear God, there are times when I feel
totally worthless, as if I just don't
matter to anyone. I feel as if no matter
what I do, it just doesn't make any
difference and that my hopes and
dreams are simply not meant to ever
come true. And so, I ask in prayer
for a new faith in your eternal and
unceasing love for me. I know that in
your eyes, I'm worthy, and I ask that
you help me realize that in my heart,
even when the world around me
makes me feel small. In your eyes, I
know that I matter. Thank you, God.

※ ※ ※

❊ ❊ ❊

In God's sight a person is the most precious of
all values. This truth possessed Jesus and
never let Him go. He thought it, taught it,
and lived it with full devotion.

—KIRBY PAGE

❊ ❊ ❊

Thank you, Lord, for making me feel
as if I'm your precious child. I may
fail at times in this world, but I know
there is a place beside you just for me
in heaven. I may make mistakes and
unintentionally hurt people, but I
know you forgive me and are always
urging me to do better. I may stumble
on my path, but I know you will
always pick me up because you love
me and because you are my God.

⁂ ⁂ ⁂

By this I know that you are pleased with me;
because my enemy has not triumphed over me.
But you have upheld me because of my integrity,
and set me in your presence forever.

—PSALM 41:11–12

❈ ❈ ❈

Father in heaven, according to your Son Jesus, each of us is a wonderful miracle of life, whom you created for a purpose. Let me understand my purpose so that my life becomes a masterpiece of living out your will in the world. Let my feet walk where you guide me, and let my voice speak the words you wish me to speak. I may often feel small, but in my heart I know you want me to love others as you love me and to be for others the beacon of hope your Son has always been for me.

❈ ❈ ❈

Lord God, I never really understood the word "joy" until I felt your love for me at work in my life. I had times of happiness, as well as exciting events that made me smile, but your love alone has touched that place deep within my heart and soul. It was then that I finally knew that true joy was present in my life. Joy is being loved by you, even when I don't really deserve it. Joy is knowing that I'm never alone and that there's always someone I can turn to for the love that passes all understanding. Joy is you, God.

❋ ❋ ❋

"Joy is the inner celebration that nothing on the outside can change the fact that God loves me."

❋ ❋ ❋

O God, I pray today for those little
reminders that you are there for me.
I pray for signs big and small that
warm my heart and tell me you are
watching over me like a loving father,
filled with concern and mercy for me.
I pray that you will show that same
concern and mercy for my family and
loved ones. When I sense your love
for me, I know that I'm deeply adored
and that you will never abandon me
in times of need.

❋ ❋ ❋

They shall again live beneath my shadow, they shall
flourish as a garden; they shall blossom like the
vine, their fragrance shall be like
the wine of Lebanon.

—HOSEA 14:7

※ ※ ※

Lord, why do I work so hard and strive to be a success at everything? Why do I always feel so empty inside, no matter what I do or achieve? Such a hollow pursuit only serves to make me feel exhausted and uninspired. I wonder for whom it is I'm living my life and to whom I have to prove myself for my sense of worth. Help me know that in your eyes I'm perfect just the way I am. Help me understand that I need not do anything or be someone special for you to love me and cherish me. This I pray, Lord. Amen.

※ ※ ※

God, put me to work and help me realize your grand purpose for my life.

I know that as your beloved child, you expect me to be the best I can be and to settle for nothing less. You have created me as a unique expression of your own love, and I long to share that expression with the world. Please empower me with everything I need to go forth and shine this little light of mine—the light you alone have given me to shine.

❈ ❈ ❈

No one after lighting a lamp puts it in a cellar, but on the lampstand so that those who enter may see the light.

—LUKE 11:33

❈ ❈ ❈

Lord God, I know that I don't have to do anything to earn your love. Just by being born, I know that you thought enough of me to give me precious life and that your love will last even after I'm gone from this world. How good it is to know that there is something in my life that never changes—that is, your love for me! I can depend upon that love and build my life into something that will make you proud to call me your child. In the precious name of Jesus, I pray. Amen.

❈ ❈ ❈

"I am a priceless masterpiece—a one-of-a-kind, unique treasure whom God loves deeply and eternally. Before I was born, he loved me. He loves me now. And when I am old and gray, he will love me still."

❊ ❊ ❊

Father God, I thank you for showing me that you love me no matter what happens and no matter how I mess up in life. I strive to do my best and to make you proud and happy, but there are those times when I just don't have enough patience or I act in a way that is inconsiderate or rude. Nevertheless, you still love me! Your acceptance of my flaws as well as my talents is what gives me joy. You love me for who I am and for who I hope to become one day in the light of your care for me. Thank you, Father God.

❊ ❊ ❊

❊ ❊ ❊

"God's grace is our comfort in times of trouble and our beacon of hope amid the darkness of despair. By opening ourselves to God's ever-present grace, we know we are loved and cared for, and our hearts sing out in joyful gratitude."

❊ ❊ ❊

Dear heavenly Father, I usually come to you in prayer to ask for help, or for guidance, or for answers to this problem or that. But today, I come to say thank you for the amazing grace you shower upon me. How can I not feel joy in my heart when you make me feel entirely loved and special and cared for? Your presence is a constant reminder that I'm precious and that my life has meaning and purpose. For that I'm truly grateful, because without meaning and purpose, life would be painfully empty. You fill me with love—for myself, for others, but mostly for you, Lord, my beloved Father!

※ ※ ※

I am like a green olive tree in the house of God.
I trust in the steadfast love of God forever and ever.
I will thank you forever, because of what you have done. In the presence of the faithful I will proclaim your name, for it is good.

—Psalm 52:8–9

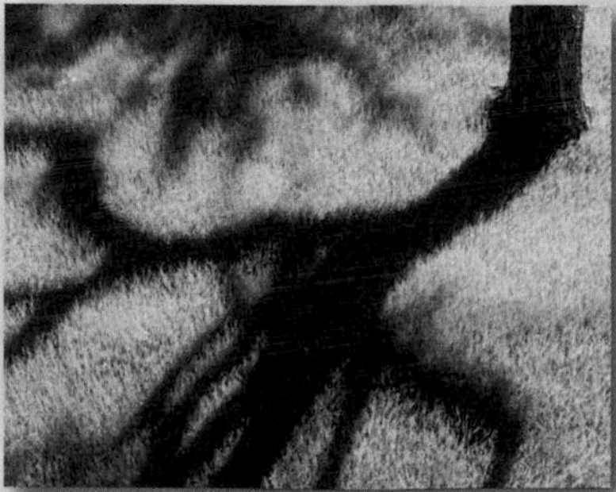

❈ ❈ ❈

Lord God, I sometimes complain and rail against your will in my life, thinking that I know better. But you know me better than I know myself, and you know that even if it hurts me now, your will is the best and highest path to a happy and purposeful future. I often lose patience with your timing, and I want things now, but you have a higher vision for my life that I can only dream of. Please forgive me when I act immaturely and impatiently. I know in my heart that your love for me is steadfast and true. I know I'm your precious child, Lord, even if on occasion I behave like a spoiled brat.

❈ ❈ ❈

✻ ✻ ✻

O Lord, I have heard of your renown, and I stand in awe, O Lord, of your work. In our own time revive it; in our own time make it known; in wrath may you remember mercy.

—Habakkuk 3:2

✻ ✻ ✻

O holy God, I'm in a lot of pain these days, and I feel unloved, lost, and alone. I feel sometimes like an abandoned child, with no one to turn to for comfort and hope. Please help me remember that you promised never to abandon me. Even though I cannot see or hear you, I know in my soul that you are present in my life, even amidst the pain and the chaos. In my narrow-minded human brain, I often focus

way too much on what I see with my
physical eyes and not enough on what
I believe. Help me find my faith again
and see with a different set of eyes that
you love me just as you always have.

❈ ❈ ❈

Be encouraged, child of God. He loves you even
in the midst of your pain. He loves you even
when you don't love Him. He loves you when
you feel utterly alone. He loves you
with an everlasting love.

—RAY PRITCHARD

❊ ❊ ❊

Today is a new day, beloved God, and a new opportunity for me to be the person you put me here to be. Today is a new chance to make better choices that reflect your love that is at work within me. It is a new opportunity to let my unique and individual light shine out into the world and serve as a vessel through which your divine love can flow out and touch others. Today is a new day for me to be the best I can be, with your love as my ever-present inspiration and your wisdom as my ever-present guide. Thank you, God, for the gift of this new day and for loving me enough to give it to me.

※ ※ ※

As you watch me from above, heavenly Father, there is nothing I need to know except that you are always close by and that your love is always with me. Just to be able to come to you in prayer makes me feel safe and secure as I face the sometimes scary world out there. With you as my loving Father, I know that I'm deeply cherished and that you will never give me anything I can't handle. I walk through my days with this deep sense of peace, and I'm filled with joy and gratitude for your presence.

※ ※ ※

"Joy is a celebration of the heart that comes from the depth of my soul. It is the knowledge

that my heavenly Father loves me and will
always take care of me."

※ ※ ※

Who can steal my joy, God, when it
is given to me by you? Who can take
away my peace? No one, because the
joy that comes from being your child
and the peace that I have with you by
my side is eternal and true. Nothing on
earth can shake my faith in you, and
nothing can ever make me doubt that
I'm cared for by a compassionate and
merciful God who never fails to come
through for me. Who can make me
doubt you are at work in my life, when
you have proven to me that you love
me in a million ways—both big and
small? Thank you, God. Amen.

※ ※ ※

God is love, and those who abide in love abide in God, and God abides in them. Love has been perfected among us in this: that we may have boldness on the day of judgment, because as he is, so are we in this world.

—1 John 4:16–17

※ ※ ※

What is grace but the love of my Savior for me! I sense your grace when I see a child smile at me, reminding me that your love is all around me. I sense your grace when something goes well, knowing that I have purpose in my life. I see your grace everywhere; it is even a part of me! Your loving care never fails, never abandons, and never ends, and I know in every fiber of my

being that I shine in your eyes and that
is all the grace I need.

※ ※ ※

*"May you know deep in your heart that God is
not in love only with what he hopes to make of
you in the years ahead; he is in love with
what you are right now—a forgiven
follower of Jesus Christ."*

❈ ❈ ❈

When you forgive me, Lord God,
I know that I'm loved by a God of
mercy and compassion and not by
a God of wrath and vengeance. You
never cease to give me a soft place to
fall when life gets a little too hard to
handle, and lately that seems to be the
case. With undying grace, you act as a
caring, doting parent ready to give me
advice and aid; yet you also give me
the freedom to make my own choices,
even my own mistakes. I know that no
matter what I do or what I accomplish
in my life, the highest achievement of
all will be my understanding of just
how loving a God you are.

❈ ❈ ❈

Dear Lord, it's been quite some time since I last turned to you for help. I know you are always there for me and that you love me as your precious child, but you know how it is. We like to think we can solve all our problems and make the right choices all by ourselves. I imagine that must make you laugh sometimes. Actually I'm not ashamed to say that I truly need you. I always need you, but today, I really could use some extra loving care and attention to help me overcome the challenges before me. I pray to you, dear Lord, with an expectant and thankful heart.

❈ ❈ ❈

This is the boldness we have in him, that if we ask anything according to his will, he hears us. And if we know that he hears us in whatever we ask, we know that we have obtained the requests made of him.

—1 John 5:14–15

❈ ❈ ❈

The sun may not come out today, and the people I love may let me down and disappoint me, but, dear God, your love never fails me. The plumbing may not work, my car may go kaput, and my mailbox may be stuffed with bills to pay, but, God, your love never fails me. No matter what I may be dealing with, I'm always able to get back to my center by just remembering that you

are my rock and my fortress—my
foundation that never shakes or
changes from beneath my feet. Thank
you, God, so very much.

⁑ ⁑ ⁑

"Always remember: God's love never fails."

⁑ ⁑ ⁑

When the cold has made my body
ache, and my legs no longer feel as
though they can carry me one more
step, I can call to you, my God, to pick
me up and carry me for a while. In
your loving and comforting arms, I
find the peace and rest I need to renew
and restore me. In your caring arms,
I am healed and strengthened so that
you can set me back down upon my

path. Thank you, God, for always having those strong and loving arms ready to carry me when I'm too tired and worn down to walk alone.

❊ ❊ ❊

Dear Lord, I sometimes feel as though I don't belong, as if I'm on the outside of my life looking in. What is your plan for me? What are your hopes for me? I ask today for your wisdom and guidance so I can live out that plan

and realize those hopes. I ask for the strength to keep on moving even when I run into a wall. I ask that you urge me on with love and inspiration when I once again feel unsure of my own footing in life, and I pray that you will show me my rightful place here on earth, as well as your will for me.

✳ ✳ ✳

If you will seek God and make supplication to the Almighty, if you are pure and upright, surely then he will rouse himself for you and restore to you your rightful place.

—JOB 8:5–6

✳ ✳ ✳

As I rise to face another day, God, I'm assured that your love will be there to greet me. I know that throughout this day there will be problems, there will be issues, and there will be drama. But just knowing how much you care for me makes me strong enough to handle anything life has to throw at me and to handle it with grace, dignity, and patience. All the drama in the world cannot shake me when my foundation is your steadfast love for me. Thank you, God.

❀ ❀ ❀

It's easy, Lord, to celebrate and be happy when all is going good as gold in my life. But for those times when my life isn't going smoothly, I have to stop and remember that everything happens for a reason and that your love is never gone or diminished. No matter what I have to deal with, you love me more than I can possibly imagine and your love for me never changes, even if I do. Life may be unstable at times, but your love, Lord, is always stable. I pray to you now to say how grateful I am for you, who saw fit to make me your beloved child and give me this amazing blessing called life.

❋ ❋ ❋

Let the peoples praise you, O God; let all the peoples praise you. The earth has yielded its increase; God, our God, has blessed us. May God continue to bless us; let all the ends of the earth revere him.

—PSALM 67:5–7

❋ ❋ ❋

❈ ❈ ❈

Dear God, can I turn to you today for help? Can I pray for a sign that you are here, always here, watching over me and protecting me? I feel a little off center and just need to know that you are with me. Knowing that is what keeps me strong and unafraid, and when I lose it, nothing seems right in my world. I know that as I sit here in quiet prayer, I will once again feel that connection. I know it is always here with me, for you never remove your

love from me. Help me remember that now.

❊ ❊ ❊

I cry to the heavens, dear God, in hopes that you will hear my small voice among many, asking for your blessings of love and strength. I am weak and need your courage. I am selfish and need your empathy and mercy. I am confused and uncertain and need your guidance and wisdom. I am alone and need your friendship and understanding. I cry to the heavens in prayer, asking that you turn your face toward me and help me make it through the day with grace and patience. In Jesus' sacred name, I pray. Amen.

CHAPTER 6

THE LORD
WILL NEVER
LEAVE ME

❈ ❈ ❈

Heavenly Father, thank you for always being with me. I'm truly grateful for the promises in your Word, the ministry of your Holy Spirit, and the fellowship of your people. Each of these blessings reveals your presence with me in a powerful way no matter what I may be going through! It's true that my feelings ebb and flow, but you are consistently strong and steadfast. I may not feel you near me at times, but the fact remains that you *are* with me. Please steady my heart and mind in this truth today.

※ ※ ※

*"When the winds of change and challenge blow
hard into my life, I take refuge in the Lord.
Although I can't see him, I know he's always with
me, and in that I take comfort and find strength."*

※ ※ ※

Dear Lord, money is not the answer
to my problems, even when I feel the
lack of it. Money goes as quickly as it
comes. Even the richest person is in
constant danger of "losing it all." But
you are the treasure that cannot be
lost or stolen. You are the one who has
made all things and to whom all things
belong. Thank you for my daily needs
that keep me tethered to your side,
reminding me that I need you and that
you are here with me. Today, Lord, I

will be content with your provisions,
as long as you are with me. How precious is your loving presence!

❊ ❊ ❊

*Keep your lives free from the love of money, and be
content with what you have; for [the Lord] has
said, "I will never leave you or forsake you." So we
can say with confidence, "The Lord is my helper; I
will not be afraid. What can anyone do to me?"*

—HEBREWS 13:5–6

❊ ❊ ❊

When I was younger, Lord God, my
feelings and circumstances were the
gauges I often used to try to discern
your demeanor toward me. Today
I see how unsound those ways of
thinking were. You have told me in
your Word what you are like and that

you are always with me. The things that are going on around me don't change who you are and what you have promised. Thank you for strengthening my faith so that I can become increasingly aware that you are always walking beside me.

※ ※ ※

Father in heaven, I know this world is not my destination; rather, it is my faith journey toward eternal life with you. Perfection and healing await me in heaven, but until then, you promise to never leave me. Even in darkness, you will be my light. Even in suffering, you will be my comfort and support. Even in death you will be my peace. And as I go through the ups and

downs of my journey here on earth
with you, I have my eyes fixed on the
goal of heaven, where my faith will
become sight, and I will see you clearly
and enjoy your presence forever.

※ ※ ※

If a person firmly believes that God is always with
him, then even if he is thrown into the depths of
the sea, he will be preserved in body and soul,
and will enjoy greater solace and comfort
than all this world can offer.

—JULIAN OF NORWICH

※ ※ ※

My Lord, even when trials and troubles cloud the landscape of my life, obscuring my view of you, let me look out with eyes of faith fixed on your promises so that my circumstances won't cause me to doubt you. I choose to put my trust in you right now, to release my worry about outcomes, and to leave those outcomes with you. I know that whatever happens, you will remain with me and will uphold me with your faithful love.

※ ※ ※

The Lord is a stronghold for the oppressed, a stronghold in times of trouble. And those who know your name put their trust in you, for you, O Lord, have not forsaken those who seek you.

—Psalm 9:9–10

❋ ❋ ❋

It doesn't matter what is troubling me, Lord, you know what I need, and I can come to you with my hurts and disappointments, as well as my fears and worries. You don't shame or chide me. Thank you for that. You're not the angry, short-tempered God some would make you out to be. Instead, you are a patient and gentle father— strong and fearless, yet tender and attentive. I could not ask for a better leader and companion in life. Even if everyone else abandons me, your presence is more than enough to see me through.

❋ ❋ ❋

❖ ❖ ❖

"The Lord does not leave us to suffer alone.
He is with us in our pain, in our sickness,
and in our worst moments."

❖ ❖ ❖

When fears of abandonment haunt
me, heavenly Father, please remind
me that everything will be all right,
because you will never leave me. The
truth is that people can be unreliable;
they may not always be there for me.
Someone may choose to walk away
from a relationship with me; friends or
family may be forced by circumstances
to move away; or death may come to
someone I love. Being left behind is
painful, Father. It's something I don't
know how to handle very well. I need

your comfort and the reassurance of
your presence with me. By your grace,
help me let go of people when I need
to, knowing that I can cling tightly to
you, the one who will never let me go.

※ ※ ※

Where were you, Lord, when I needed
you? When I lost my loved one to
illness? When I went bankrupt?
When I was abused and cheated and
powerless? Where were you? It felt
as if you were nowhere to be found.
It felt as if you had abandoned me. I
wondered if you even cared. Where
were you? That's how I felt when it
was happening. But now, I know the
answer. You were with me. I came
through it with a new understanding,

with a deeper empathy for those who suffer, and with a strengthened faith. I realize now that you were taking care of me, even in those dark times. You never left me, and you never will. Thank you, Lord. Thank you.

※ ※ ※

"Faith flows when I stop depending on what I think, on what I feel, and on what I see. Instead, I embrace these facts: God loves me. He will never leave me. He wants only the best for me."

❈ ❈ ❈

The old gospel song "Take My Hand,
Precious Lord" expresses my need
for you extremely well, Lord God. I
understand that it was written during
a time of deep sorrow. Please hear it as
my prayer today, Lord, as I pour out
the troubles in my heart to you. How
I need the assurance of your presence
with me right now! How I need you to
cradle my heart and heal it! Hold me
up, I pray, even though I feel as though
I will fall and never rise again. Hold
my hand securely in yours, Lord. I
pray in Jesus' name. Amen.

❈ ❈ ❈

*Our steps are made firm by the Lord, when
he delights in our way; though we stumble,*

*we shall not fall headlong, for the Lord
holds us by the hand.*

—Psalm 37:23–24

※ ※ ※

Since you are everywhere at all times,
Lord God, there is no way you could
ever not be with me. But your Word
speaks of a more meaningful way in
which you are with me—a personal
and intimate fellowship that you bring
to my life. It is for this loving way you
come alongside me that I praise you
today. You are, indeed, the almighty
God of the universe, who is all knowing and present everywhere at once
and who sees me and has initiated
an eternal friendship with me. What
a reason to rejoice today, Lord!

❈ ❈ ❈

Abiding in your presence, Father in heaven, is my "safe place" when everything seems to have gone sideways. When people are angry with me, when my insecurities rise up, when I've been a jerk, and when I've not been faithful to what I know is right and true and good—these are the times when I want to hide from everyone and sometimes even from you, Lord. But you invite me to come and be forgiven, encouraged, renewed, and reminded of your love for me within the protection of your loving presence. No matter what I'm dealing with right now, Lord, I will hide myself under your wings.

❈ ❈ ❈

※ ※ ※

Under his wings I am safely abiding, though the night deepens and tempests are wild; still I can trust him, I know he will keep me, he has redeemed me and I am his child.

—William O. Cushing

※ ※ ※

Even in lean times, my Creator, you provide for those who walk with you. You are the source of all provision, and to walk with you is to have all I need. Sometimes you have fortified my faith by having me wait on you, and in your timing you have always come through with food, shelter, finances, and clothing when I've been in need of them. Sometimes you have redirected me by withholding what I thought I needed, but that was also part of your provision, a provision of guidance. Thank you for taking such good care of me as I walk with you. You have never forsaken me, not once.

※ ※ ※

I have been young, and now am old, yet I have not seen the righteous forsaken or their children begging bread. They are ever giving liberally and lending, and their children become a blessing.

—Psalm 37:25–26

❈ ❈ ❈

Sometimes I act as if I can boss you around, Lord, but it's foolish of me to think and act that way. Sometimes I get all out of sorts when you don't do things the way I think you should, and I'm sorry for behaving that way toward you. I often need to be reminded that you are sovereign, that you are in charge, and that you know exactly how things will happen. My job is to trust in you, to wait patiently for you, and to find peace in these postures of faith. You are always with me; you are always faithful; and you are always good. I need never doubt you.

❈ ❈ ❈

❊ ❊ ❊

"No one knows the mind of God, nor why he chooses to work the way he does. But in our most difficult circumstances, we will miss the peace of his presence unless we persevere in trusting that he is always faithful and always good."

❊ ❊ ❊

How peacefully a beloved child or cherished pet sleeps when they know we are near! May I trust your nearness to me in that same way, dear Lord. May I lie down and sleep well, knowing you are here. May I awake and feel safe and secure knowing you go before me into the fray of each day. May I quickly consult your wisdom when difficulties arise. May I stop to praise you when I experience your blessings. May

I always be aware of your presence
with me and lean into you with trust,
love, and gratitude. Amen.

❈ ❈ ❈

Dear Lord, you are the best of friends.
I could never find the kind of solace
I find in you anywhere else. When
I'm troubled and flailing about in my
distress, I sometimes flit about from
person to person, seeking comfort and
help. But then, when I've worn myself
out with this anxious activity, there
you are, quietly waiting for me, ready
to wrap your love and peace around
me and take me into the place of
comfort and assurance. Thank you for
being here for me without fail and for
your goodness to me today.

※ ※ ※

The salvation of the righteous is from the Lord; he is
their refuge in the time of trouble. The Lord helps
them and rescues them; he rescues them from
the wicked and saves them, because they
take refuge in him.

—Psalm 37:39–40

※ ※ ※

Thank you, heavenly Father, that when
I have "ugly days"—when I'm out of
sorts and don't even like being in my
own skin—you don't turn away from
me in disgust. Sometimes I have a hard
time believing you are still here with
me after the way I've behaved. Every
time I come to my senses and turn my
heart to seek you in prayer for help
and forgiveness, you are with me. And

when I come to you, I don't find a toe-tapping, tsk-tsking Father, but rather, one who reminds me of his love for me and who is happy I have come to him to get cleaned up and back on track. I'm blessed to be your child and to have you as my eternal Father.

❈ ❈ ❈

My Lord, how often human love fails, my own included! Our so-called love is usually made of different stuff than yours is. We often fashion our love gifts for one another like Trojan horses, filled with expectations of something we'll get in return. Sadly, Lord, too many of my love offerings to others are merely a selfish imitation of your selfless, eternal love for me. Please teach me to love as you love, for your love always protects, always hopes, and always perseveres. Truly, it never fails. Thank you for your ever-present, unfailing love.

"Rejoice! For God's love never fails."

※ ※ ※

From youth to old age, Lord God, you
remain with those who walk with you.
You never take vacations from your
children. You never hire a babysitter.
You never run out on us or leave us
with relatives. You stay with us, not as
an obligation, but as one who cherishes
and delights in us. What a wonderful
thing to consider! I'm not a burden or
a hassle to you, Lord; you *like* being
with me. And it's not because of anything special I do; it's because you are
so thoroughly good and kind, tender-
hearted and merciful toward your
children. How wonderful you are!
How wonderful it is to walk with you
my whole life through!

❈ ❈ ❈

O God, from my youth you have taught me, and I still proclaim your wondrous deeds. So even to old age and gray hairs, O God, do not forsake me, until I proclaim your might to all the generations to come.

—Psalm 71:17–18

❈ ❈ ❈

When I feel alone, dear Lord, remind me that I'm never alone because you are always with me. When I feel lonely, let me open my heart to your friendship. When I'm rejected, flood my soul with a deep sense of your acceptance. When I fail, let me be quick to seek your comfort and forgiveness. When I'm in awe of your creation, let praise flow from my lips toward you. Whenever, wherever, whatever I may be experiencing in life, Lord, may I instinctively turn toward you to find you with me, ready to engage with me in the moment and being everything that I need and long for.

Almighty God, someone has said that we should never doubt in the darkness what you have shown us in the light. But the intensity of darkness some-times causes me to forget what I've seen in the light. Truly, I could never navigate this darkness without you here with me to remind me of what is true! I could never venture out into the unknown if I did not know you were with me—you, the all-knowing one! And if I look at anything or anyone but you as the uncertainty of the future looms ahead, I quickly lose heart. But as I keep my eyes on you, my hand in yours, I confidently go forward.

※ ※ ※

"The Lord gives me the faith to take the next step, even when I don't know what lies ahead. He gives me the assurance that even if my faith falters, he will never abandon me."

※ ※ ※

Thank you, Lord, for your grace, love, and fellowship. Thank you for all the ways you minister to all my needs—spiritual, emotional, and social. Today, when I sense my need for grace, I will turn to you and find you here. When I need love, here you will be ready to assure me of your own. When I need fellowship and friendship, here your Spirit will be ministering and communing with me. How grateful I am that I am never without what my heart and soul need because you are always with me! Amen.

※ ※ ※

It has taken some time for me to understand that you will never leave me, Lord. I tend to project onto you my own tendencies or the things I have experienced at the hands of others. Please forgive me for thinking of you in these terms. You don't deserve my doubt and suspicion, but you have patiently endured my fears and misplaced accusations until I have understood the truth about your faithful love for me. Thank you for not giving up, for being kind when I was not, and for being gentle when I was angry and quick to judge your timing and ways. I was slow to learn, but now I place trust in the certainty that you are with me and will never fail me.

※ ※ ※

*"Comfort comes to God's people
in their times of need."*

※ ※ ※

Bless you, Lord God! Bless you for
your goodness to your children! Bless
you for never leaving or forsaking us!
Bless you for loving us without our
having to earn your love! My heart is
full of thanks and praise because you
are with me. My soul has a deep and
abiding security because you will never
leave me. My spirit rejoices because
you have brought me near to you
through your great salvation. I am
richly blessed. Receive my praise, dear
Father! May such praise bless your
heart today.

CHAPTER 7

GOD CARRIES ME THROUGH TRIALS

❊❊ ❊❊ ❊❊

Lord God, I often wonder why we have to struggle so much and feel so much pain in life. In my case, I know it must be for my own good, but I do wish it would end soon. And since I find it hard to deal with it on my own, I come to you in prayer today to ask for your help. With your strength, I know I can handle this present pain, knowing that this, too, shall pass. I just don't think I can do it alone, Lord. Please let me lean on you today.

❈ ❈ ❈

In that day, says the Lord, I will assemble the lame and gather those who have been driven away, and those whom I have afflicted. The lame I will make the remnant, and those who were cast off, a strong nation.

—Micah 4:6–7

❈ ❈ ❈

It seems really dark outside, God, even though the sun is shining and the sky is clear. I have a lot on my mind and so many things to think about. I'm also feeling lost and alone without a friend in the world. I need someone stronger than I am to carry me through these trials, and I know that your loving arms provide just the right comfort and strength to make me feel as

though I can do anything. God, walk
with me today, just in case my feet fail
me. I know you will be there to catch
me when I fall. Thank you, God.

❈ ❈ ❈

*"In the midst of our troubles, God comes to us.
In the darkness, His Spirit moves,
spreading light like a shower of stars breaking
through a stormy night sky."*

❈ ❈ ❈

I pray to you today, heavenly Father,
to thank you for the constant and
reassuring presence you have become
in my life. I remember a time when
I tried really hard to go it alone, and
wow, what a mess I made of things!
But knowing that you are always
beside me, during bad times and good,

helps me feel secure even in the most insecure of situations. I cannot tell you what a difference that has made in my life, but then, I imagine you know my own soul. Thank you, Father.

※ ※ ※

Dear God, I have heard people say when one door closes, another door opens in its place. Today I ask in prayer that I may see that new opportunity for happiness open up to me. I have knocked, and my heart is now tired and hurt, and I'm in need of a new hope to carry on. Please be the strength that I do not have, and please provide me with the faith I struggle to believe in when all doors around me seem to be closed. I know that you will

open one, and I ask in prayer that it be
soon. Amen.

✳ ✳ ✳

*"My strength and my weakness are in the Lord's
hands. He preserves my strength and helps
my weakness. Where the door is shut,
he will open at my knocking."*

✳ ✳ ✳

I'm thankful, Lord, that when I'm too
weak, you give me strength and, when
I'm too tired, you infuse me with new
energy. I'm thankful that when I'm too
frightened, you give me courage to
move forward in the face of fear. I'm
thankful that when I'm confused, you
show me a clear vision and a direction
with purpose. For so many things I'm

thankful, Lord, because when I'm facing the impossible, your presence makes all things possible.

※ ※ ※

As for me, I would seek God, and to God I would commit my cause. He does great things and unsearchable, marvelous things without number. He gives rain on the earth and sends waters on the fields; he sets on high those who are lowly, and those who mourn are lifted to safety.

—Job 5:8–11

❈ ❈ ❈

Dear Father in heaven, as your faithful child, I know that I can turn to you for the courage I lack when I'm in need of it. I pray today for a little extra courage and perhaps even a bit of patience. I'm being challenged and don't want to lose my cool and react in anger, because when I do there is never anything good that can come from it. Please help me keep my temper in check, my tongue in place, and my heart calm as I deal with my challenges today. With your help, I know I can make things right again.

❈ ❈ ❈

I do not fear the dark, Lord, when I know that I have you as my shining light to guide me. I do not shudder from the cold, Lord, when I feel your constant presence warming me. I do not back down from challenges, Lord, when I sense you standing beside me, ready to offer me your strength and fortitude. Nothing can shake my faith in you, for you are my rock, my fortress, and my comforting balm in times of trouble. You are my light, my guide, and my director in this play called my life. Thank you, Lord.

※ ※ ※

Whom have I in heaven but you? And there is nothing on earth that I desire other than you. My flesh and my heart may fail, but God is the strength of my heart and my portion forever.

—PSALM 73:25–26

※ ※ ※

O God, I'm truly grateful to have you
as my rock to stand upon and my soft
place to fall should I stumble along the
way. You provide me with strength
when I need it and gentle loving care
when I need that, too. There is nothing
here on earth that can fill the emptiness inside me but you, O God. I'm
always whole and always at peace
because of your love for me, and for
that I am truly grateful.

※ ※ ※

*"Sometimes emotional or psychological pain can
burn so deep within me that it scorches the center
of my soul, bringing me utter darkness and
despair. Yet even in this most terrible pain, I can
turn to the Lord for courage, comfort, strength,*

and the victory he lovingly offers me, while giving
me light and hope to see me through."

❋ ❋ ❋

When the weight of my despair
threatens to pull me under, I know
that you, Lord, will take me by the
hand and pull me out of the deep
waters and place me upon dry land.
No matter how much I cry and hurt,
I feel a place deep within where you
reside, and I know that these painful
times will pass and that I will heal
with time and patience and your love.
I would rather not go through this
pain, but I do so with confidence and
faith that it is for my spiritual growth
and that I will come out the other side
a stronger and better person. Amen.

※ ※ ※

So we do not lose heart. Even though our outer nature is wasting away, our inner nature is being renewed day by day. For this slight momentary affliction is preparing us for an eternal weight of glory beyond all measure.

—2 Corinthians 4:16–17

※ ※ ※

Dear heavenly Father, just as you have been a source of strength for me, please become that source for my family and friends. So many of my loved ones seem to be going through such awful challenges lately, and I don't always know the best way to help them. Guide me to say and do just the right things to help them feel stronger and more capable so that they can rise up and meet their problems with newfound faith and fortitude. Just as you are a light in my life, Father, let me now be that light for others wherever and whenever I can. I pray in Jesus' name. Amen.

※ ※ ※

"God meets us in our weakness and turns our weakness into strength."

❊ ❊ ❊

My Lord, let me lean on you for a
while. I have little strength left right
now and my hopes have faded. Let me
find some comfort in your love and
your guidance. I will surrender my
thoughts and my will to you, and I will
stop trying to fix everything. I will let
you guide me to the right way to repair
all that is broken in my life. Let me
rest with you awhile. I'm tired and
want a little peace in my life right now.
I don't ask that you lift these difficulties from my life, only that you help
me get through them.

❊ ❊ ❊

Expect periods of hardship to occur, and don't be
dismayed when they arrive. Lean into the pain

when your time to suffer comes around, knowing
that God will use the difficulty for his purpose—
and indeed, for our own good.

—JAMES DOBSON

※ ※ ※

Holy God, you have chosen to bless
me with so many material things, but
today I want to thank you for those
immaterial things that mean even
more to me. You have blessed me with
faith and hope in things unseen. You
have blessed me with love for my
family, for my friends, and for the
world. You have blessed me with
strength, patience, and tolerance when
dealing with others. You have blessed
me with a sense of humor and humility. I could go on and on listing the
blessings you've bestowed upon me.

For now, let me just say thank you, thank you, thank you!

❈ ❈ ❈

When the hard rains fall, dear Lord, you are like the umbrella that shields me from the cold and the harshness of the storm. You are the sun that comes out afterward to warm my heart again and bring life to all that was dead inside me. I know that suffering is a part of life, but I don't have to like it. I do accept it, though, knowing that it is helping me grow and become stronger and more resilient. Please keep that umbrella handy, dear Lord. I never know when I might need you. Yes, I do know—I always need you.

❈ ❈ ❈

Come, let us return to the Lord; for it is he who has torn, and he will heal us; he has struck down, and he will bind us up. After two days he will revive us; on the third day he will raise us up, that we may live before him.

—HOSEA 6:1–2

❈ ❈ ❈

I hate being a needy child, but you are my loving Father, and I come to you for the comfort and strength only a loving parent can provide. My courage is sorely lacking lately, heavenly Father, and I ask that you be my courage right now, just long enough to help me make it to the other side of this dark valley before me. I do not want to walk that valley alone, so please take my hand as

a parent takes the hand of a child, and
help me find that sure and steady path.

❋ ❋ ❋

*"If we would stop pretending to be strong, start
being honest with ourselves and God, and cry
out, 'God, please help! I am poor and needy,'
he would hurry to help us and be
the strength of our lives."*

❈ ❈ ❈

Dear God, how you must laugh when we pretend that we are so strong and brave, and yet inside we are shaking and trembling like a frightened animal! But instead, you show us mercy and grace by supplying us with the strength and courage we lack so that we can stand tall against any enemy—real or imagined. How we must seem so silly to you with our petty problems! But instead, you show us love and compassion and make us feel loved, cared for, and protected. Thank you, God.

❈ ❈ ❈

Thus says the Lord of hosts: If you will walk in my ways and keep my

requirements, then you shall rule my
house and have charge of my courts,
and I will give you the right of access
among those who are standing here.

—ZECHARIAH 3:6–7

※ ※ ※

I find it really hard to just let go and
surrender my problems to you, my
heavenly Creator. I know you can
handle them far better than I can, but
I guess the control freak in me is really
strong. Please help me learn how to
let it all go and to trust in your ability
to handle the things I just can't seem
to get a grip on lately. Please, Lord,
strengthen my faith and give me the
courage to put my problems squarely
where they belong—in your loving and
caring hands.

❈ ❈ ❈

"Let go and let God see you through."

❈ ❈ ❈

Loving Father above, do my problems
seem petty from your perspective? To
me they're big and scary, like demons
I struggle with daily. Help me find
the higher vision so that I can see the
bigger picture you see. I ask for your
strength where mine comes up short
and for your wisdom where mine is
sadly inadequate. I know in my heart
that you have planned a purposeful life
for me. Just help me see that higher
purpose so I can move beyond the
day-to-day problems with courage,
faith, and hope.

❊ ❊ ❊

Then the eyes of the blind shall be opened, and the ears of the deaf unstopped; then the lame shall leap like a deer, and the tongue of the speechless sing for joy.

—ISAIAH 35:5–6

❊ ❊ ❊

Thank you, thank you, and thank you, God, for doing for me what I can't do for myself. It seems that each and every time when I say to myself, "How can I get through this?" you provide me with the courage, strength, and determination I need, not to mention your guidance and direction. Your love and attention never fail me, even when my family and friends are not here for me. I know that I can depend upon you and you alone to never let me down, and for that I'm more and more grateful each day. People in my life may come and go, but you, God, are my rock and my hope forever. Amen.

※ ※ ※

My Lord, I usually ask you for things that are material—things like more money to pay the bills, nicer clothes to wear, a bigger house in which to live, and a more reliable car to drive. But, in truth, I know that the greatest gifts you give me are worth far more than all of those things put together. I can survive with little if I know that you are in my world, for you are a constant, loving presence that I can turn to and walk with at anytime. Your strength and love are what make life worth living, not all those other things. With you in my life, I know that I will live, and live abundantly, in all the ways that really matter.

❊ ❊ ❊

One ounce of God's strength is worth
more than all the world.

—Dwight L. Moody

❊ ❊ ❊

Father in heaven, I pray to you today
for help and hope, both of which are
in short supply in my life. I need help
moving beyond the drama and issues
I can't seem to ever resolve, and I need
the hope to believe there is a light at
the end of this long, dark tunnel. You
have helped me through so many
trying times that I know you won't let
me down, but hurry with that help
and hope soon. I'm at the end of my
rope and need your love to hang onto.

❈ ❈ ❈

Blessed be the name of God from age to age, for wisdom and power are his. He changes times and seasons, deposes kings and sets up kings; he gives wisdom to the wise and knowledge to those who have understanding.

—Daniel 2:20–21

※ ※ ※

Dear Lord, you are my nightlight when I'm afraid of the dark. You are my comforting blanket when I'm cold and shivering. I thank you for all that you are to me. I thank you most of all for the peace I have in knowing that no matter what goes on, you are here to lead me through it. I have nothing to fear with you as my loving Father, and everything to believe in and hope for. Thank you, Lord.

※ ※ ※

"In the midst of the darkness that threatens to overwhelm us lies a pinpoint of light—a persistent flicker that guides us through the pain and fear, through the hopelessness and despair, to a place of peace and healing on the other side.

This is God's Spirit, leading us back home like the lighthouse beacon that directs the ships through the fog to the safety of the harbor."

❋ ❋ ❋

O God, I follow your light as I walk through my dark valleys. Sometimes your light seems so dim that you appear far away, and so I rest in my faith knowing that if I keep moving in the right direction, you will be there to meet me halfway. I ask in prayer that you continue to show me the way to peace and joy and to be the strength that I often can't find within myself. I do see your light, dear God, calling me forward. And faithfully I will follow you wherever you take me.

※ ※ ※

The light is with you for a little longer. Walk while you have the light, so that the darkness may not overtake you. If you walk in the darkness, you do not know where you are going. While you have the light, believe in the light, so that you may become children of light.

—JOHN 12:35–36

※ ※ ※

Father, who but you is my fortress and my strength? I can lean on my loved ones for only so long, but they have fears and problems of their own. You, though, never deny me the love and care I seek. You never turn away from me in times of need or despair, no matter how angry and impatient I become. What a blessing it is to know

that I can always count on you to be
there when no one around me can be
counted on! Thank you for your steadfast presence and faithfulness to me.

❋ ❋ ❋

Lord God, I sing out today to tell the
world that you are the rock upon
which my feet hold fast and the fortress behind which I'm safe from all
the storms and battles of life. I sing
out today to tell the world about your
undying love for me, your work in me,
and the blessings you shower upon
me each time I come to you as your
beloved child. Hear my song of happiness and gratitude, God, for I sing out
today to thank you for everything you
have done for me.

❊ ❊ ❊

My lips will shout for joy when I sing praises to you; my soul also, which you have rescued. All day long my tongue will talk of your righteous help.

—PSALM 71:23–24

❊ ❊ ❊

Dear heavenly Father, I'm your child—your beloved child here on earth. Please work through me, so I can help others as you have helped me. I want to be like you in every way, using your strength and your wisdom to work miracles in other people's lives, even as you continue to work miracles in my life. I also want to be your faithful child, so you can be a light in the world through me. I pray in Jesus' holy name. Amen.

CHAPTER 8

PRAY EVEN
IN THE
MIDST OF
DOUBTS

❈ ❈ ❈

Heavenly Father, you have taught me
that you would rather hear a tirade
of honest frustration from me than
a litany of false devotion. As one
psalmist wrote, you are the God who
desires "truth in the inward parts." So,
Lord, help me as I work through my
thoughts of feeling let down by you.
When things don't go the way I want,
I sometimes feel as if you aren't here
for me. So I'll pour my disappointments in prayer, knowing that you
already know all about my doubts but
also that you invite me to come to you
and tell you what's in my heart.

❈ ❈ ❈

❊ ❊ ❊

"Even when we falsely blame God for our disappointments, he is always ready to listen to our complaints. How great is his mercy and love toward us!"

❊ ❊ ❊

You may be working out another plan, Lord God, but I can't see that at this moment. In fact, it feels as if everything that can go wrong has gone wrong. I can't fathom what you're doing. Why don't you help me? How long do I have to wait until I get some relief? Are you even listening to me? I believe you are, but your silence baffles me. I know that you're not indifferent, but that's what it feels like while I desperately need your help. My faith needs a lift, so I'm asking you once again, Lord. Please help me. Please help my unbelief!

❈ ❈ ❈

You will be in the right, O Lord, when I lay charges against you; but let me put my case to you.

—JEREMIAH 12:1

❈ ❈ ❈

Maybe my disappointment is a small thing in the scope of eternity, but it's a big thing to me right now, Lord. I had hoped for a different outcome, but it just didn't happen that way. I had prayed for your intervention, but it didn't come—at least, not in the way I had hoped. I had wanted things to turn out for the best, but now everything seems to have fallen apart. I

don't want to feel anger toward you,
but I do right now. I believe it will pass
and you will help me find perspective
on all of this, but until then, I need
your grace and mercy to help me move
toward that place of acceptance, trust,
and peace.

❈ ❈ ❈

I thought that following you, God, would make my life far easier, but I see that's not really the case. In fact, this process of building my faith is down-right painful at times. Sometimes I wish I could just stop and go with the flow, take the path of least resistance, and forget this narrow road that leads to life. But I don't really want to aban-don the path and stop following you. Please help me though these growing pains. I really need your grace and strength. Thank you, God, for being with me and for nurturing me.

❈ ❈ ❈

"God answers our prayers in his own way. If his answers disappoint you, remember that he often

uses adversity to reveal that he is our refuge and strength, a very present help in trouble."

✺ ✺ ✺

Sometimes, Lord, it feels as though you're against me instead of for me. I know your Word says, "If God is for us, who can be against us?" But when it seems as though your hand is against me, what am I to make of it? It's miserable, and I just want you to leave me alone and stop bringing so much hardship my way. I know you could stop it. Why don't you? Are you angry with me? Is there sin you are trying to point out to me? What do I need to do to cause you to quit heaping troubles on me? O God, please come and comfort me. Show me what you mean by all of these hardships. I long to understand what's going on, and I long to feel that you are, indeed, still "for me."

❈ ❈ ❈

I loathe my life; I will give free utterance to my complaint; I will speak in the bitterness of my soul. I will say to God, Do not condemn me; let me know why you contend against me.

—Job 10:1–2

✼ ✼ ✼

Why, Lord, when I have tried to be good to others and do right by them, do they return evil for my kindness? Backstabbing, betrayal, slander, rejection, any and all of it is deeply hurtful to me. I care about others. I really do. I don't wish any ill on them. Meanwhile, I detest mocking and mean-spiritedness. And yet I find these arrows flying my way from people I have tried hard to love in the way you would have me do. I'm smarting from these wounds, Lord. Please help me heal and help me not to become bitter, even though I feel so angry. Renew my love, I pray.

✼ ✼ ✼

"Persistent prayer is the greatest act of faith."

❊ ❊ ❊

Thank you, Lord, for not rejecting my prayers to you when they are full of frustration and weariness. I don't want to be a chronic complainer, treating you like the Complaint Department, but I do want to talk to you about what concerns me today. I will lay out my troubles before you and put them into your hands. Please renew my heart, soul, mind, and strength even now so that, despite my trials, I will truly live full of my love for you.

❊ ❊ ❊

With my voice I cry to the Lord; with my voice I make supplication to the Lord. I pour out my complaint before him; I tell my trouble before him. When my spirit is faint, you know my way.

—Psalm 142:1–3

❈ ❈ ❈

Heavenly Father, I don't know why you continue to withhold the deepest desire of my heart. You must have a reason, but all I know is that I keep longing, and you keep saying no. It feels as if you're rejecting me when I see others around me getting the things they want, and especially when you grant them the very thing for which I've been asking. It hurts deeply, and I don't know how to understand it. Help me trust your wisdom, your plan, and most importantly, your love for me.

"When we expect God to respond to our problems exactly as we desire, we will frequently be disappointed. More often than not, God does not think the way we think."

❈ ❈ ❈

Oppressive people, difficult situations, and unwanted thoughts eclipse my peace and joy, Lord. I feel cornered and trapped when these things rise up against me. I'm not equal to them in my own strength. I feel defeated and depressed when they come marching out to meet me. Please fight for me, Lord! Train me to stand up with you in truth and love and to send these enemies of my soul packing. I can be joyful and peaceful when I fully entrust myself to you.

❊ ❊ ❊

The Lord is a stronghold for the oppressed, a stronghold in times of trouble. And those who know your name put their trust in you, for you, O Lord, have not forsaken those who seek you.

—Psalm 9:9–10

❊ ❊ ❊

I've heard it said that we should be thankful that you don't give us everything we ask for, Father. I can look back and see that that's true when I consider some of the things you've withheld from me when I thought I knew what would be best for me. Some reasons for your "no" answers aren't so apparent, though. It's harder to give thanks for those times, but I will thank you anyway today for keeping me from unseen disasters, miseries, and regrets. And I'll trust you, even though I feel disappointed and saddened when your answer to my desperate pleas are met with a wisdom beyond my own that lovingly but firmly says, "No, child."

❈ ❈ ❈

Keep praying, but be thankful that God's answers
are wiser than your prayers.

—WILLIAM CULBERTSON

❈ ❈ ❈

Dear Lord God, when I'm struggling,
your "no" responses are not nearly
as difficult to accept as your silence.
What does it mean when you leave me
waiting in the deafening stillness after
I have poured out my heart to you?
Where are you when I need to feel you
near, but it seems you are really far off
somewhere? I would rather hear you
say *anything* to me, even if it's something that will be painful to hear than
to have you answer me with a stone
wall of silence. Perhaps it is not that

you are being silent. Maybe I'm just not tuned in to hear what you are saying. In any case, please grant me the understanding to know what I need to perceive.

❈ ❈ ❈

Today also my complaint is bitter; his hand is heavy despite my groaning. Oh, that I knew where I might find him, that I might come even to his dwelling! I would lay my case before him, and fill my mouth with arguments. I would learn what he would answer me, and understand what he would say to me.

—Job 23:1–5

❊ ❊ ❊

In my prayers, I have brought my praises to you, along with my requests, confessions, and complaints, Lord. You have always welcomed me into your presence to tell you what is on my heart and mind. Thank you for having an open door for your children to come to you with their bundles of thoughts, feelings, concerns, and needs. I don't know what I would do without your invitation to boldly come into your throne room of grace—to find grace and mercy in time of need. Help me avail myself of your invitation! I pray in Jesus' name. Amen.

❊ ❊ ❊

❊ ❊ ❊

I think that the presence of evil and
suffering in the world is the hardest
thing to understand about life and
about your permissive will, Lord.
People sometimes ask me, when I tell
them that I trust in you, "How can a
loving God allow children to suffer?"
What shall I say, Lord? You do allow
it. I know you do not desire it and that
it's our own departure from your good
ways that invites and creates suffering.
And one day you will do away with all
suffering and evil, but until that time,
Lord, we coexist with it, and it's hard
to perceive why you allow it. Help me
be your hands and feet, your heart and
voice to those who suffer so that they
can understand that your perfect will

is for healing and wholeness and for
life and love.

❋ ❋ ❋

*"If we believe that God causes our suffering, we
need to turn to the Bible to learn that God is our
creator, savior, healer, and protector."*

❋ ❋ ❋

I can see how, over time, my disappointments have helped bring me
a more mature perspective, Lord. It
makes perfect sense when I look at
parent-child relationships here on
earth. Children who are indulged,
given everything they want, and are
pampered and coddled are naturally
self-centered. Their perspective has
never been broadened to take in the

considerations of others. What a tragedy it would be if you treated your own children that way! So thank you for the adversity and disappointment that has come my way from your hand. I have learned to trust you and love others in ways I would not otherwise have known.

※ ※ ※

We are afflicted in every way, but not crushed; perplexed, but not driven to despair; persecuted, but not forsaken; struck down, but not destroyed.

—2 Corinthians 4:8–9

※ ※ ※

Heavenly Father, losing loved ones is agonizing. I know death is not final and that you have promised resurrection for all and eternal life for those who love you. But this life is where I still am, and saying goodbye is sometimes crushing. The grief engulfs and overwhelms me, and only time can heal it. But time moves slowly when grief is with me. I wish death didn't have to come and steal away the people I love. But it does, and one day it will steal me away. O God! Please be my comfort and my steady hope. I trust in you. Amen.

※ ※ ※

"I prayed but received no answer; I believed but nothing changed; I waited and grew anxious. And so, I went to God to help my failing faith!"

※ ※ ※

In the wee hours, Lord, when I can't sleep because my heart and mind are troubled, you hear my prayers. I keep asking you to help me, to give me wisdom and insight, to provide and protect, and to rescue me and restore peace. I pray because I cannot help it. Who else should I ask for help? Who else is able to intervene for me? Only you. And then in the stark reality of daytime, the issues about which I called out to you are still before me. I wonder how and when you will respond. I wait and wonder. O Lord, please don't make me wait forever!

※ ※ ※

I, O Lord, cry out to you; in the morning my prayer comes before you. O Lord, why do you cast me off? Why do you hide your face from me?

—PSALM 88:13–14

※ ※ ※

Dear Father, why do natural disasters happen in the world? Earthquakes, floods, famine, hurricanes, and disease plague our world and wreak havoc on humanity. What purpose can these disasters possibly serve? Isn't it enough that we suffer from the normal strife of living and dying? Must these horrific disasters swallow people's lives, and especially the lives of babies and little children? But then I see your compassion flow from those who come to help and heal when these disasters strike. I hear that people are sometimes better off than they were before after the relief flows in from around the world. I don't understand all your ways, but I see you at work in the world, transforming tragedy into a sort of saving grace. Show me how I can cooperate with you in this—to bring your love and compassion to those who are suffering today.

✻ ✻ ✻

You're a convenient target for blame,
Lord, when things don't go right. It
happens more than I want to admit
that I turn an accusing look your way
when I'm not happy with how things
are shaping up. I think, *Why did you let
this happen?* or *Why didn't you do it this
way?* or *What am I supposed to do now
that you've wrecked my plan?* If only
I praised you for all of my blessings
as much as I chide you for all of my
frustrations! Help me, Lord, to blame
you less and praise you more.

✻ ✻ ✻

*"When we fail to trust God, we blame him for
our struggles. So believe in him, and never
lose faith in the Lord."*

※ ※ ※

Trouble will come to me in this world;
you've told me this in your Word,
Lord. But it can still sometimes take
me by surprise and make me lose sleep
when I have to deal with unexpected
trouble in my life. You've said I need
not worry because you have overcome
the world, but it's difficult not to
worry when I'm feeling overcome *by*
the world. Troublesome people and
circumstances are stealing my joy.
Please help me rest in you today, Lord.
I pray in your name. Amen.

※ ※ ※

*In the day of my trouble I seek the Lord; in the night
my hand is stretched out without wearying; my soul
refuses to be comforted. I think of God, and I moan;*

I meditate, and my spirit faints.... Has God forgotten to be gracious?

—Psalm 77:2–3, 9

※ ※ ※

How am I supposed to love these unlovely people in my life, Lord? They can make my day go south faster than any other problem I face. I hate it when my day is going well and one of them comes and turns everything sour with a terrible attitude and discouraging words. I just want to run when I see such people coming. If only I could! Please show me how to shake off the residue of these encounters and resume a spirit of peace and joy. Help me remember to pray for these people. They need your love too.

❋ ❋ ❋

"We prayed but didn't feel answered. Looking back now, however, we realize God did answer but in his own profound way."

❋ ❋ ❋

When my soul is parched, O God, when my prayers seem as if they're simply echoing into empty space, revive my spirit with your Word. Uplift me by helping me to hope again in your promises. Remind me of your perfect track record of faithfulness so that I won't lose heart and stop lifting my voice to you. If you didn't encourage me during those times, almighty God, I think I would lapse into despair, but your Word is always within reach, and your Spirit is always

here to help me understand and
believe what is written in your Word.

✳ ✳ ✳

*Hear my prayer, O Lord; let my cry come to you.
Do not hide your face from me in the day of my
distress. Incline your ear to me; answer me speedily
in the day when I call.... My heart is stricken
and withered like grass.*

—Psalm 102:1–2, 4

※ ※ ※

When I pleaded with you, Lord, for that thing I believed would make me truly happy, and you didn't comply, remember how angry I was? I was really mad at you! But you held your ground and loved me, even in my tantrum. It was when I perceived how destructive that thing would have been in my life that I knew you loved me and would rather have me angry for a season than hurt for a lifetime. Thank you for loving me so much.

※ ※ ※

I call upon God and the Lord will save me. Evening and morning and at noon I utter my complaint and moan, and he will hear my voice.

—PSALM 55:16–17

❈ ❈ ❈

Though my valleys may be deep and long, Lord, yet you are here with me. When the path before me is steep and treacherous, please help me remember that you will strengthen me and keep me safe. The sun may not shine for many days on end, but remind me that you are my light and my salvation. The rain may fall and the wind may blow, but if you tell me that you are my shelter and my comfort, I will not be dismayed. Though I encounter many trials and troubles along the way, Lord, you are truly my everything, and I will put my trust in you. In Jesus' sacred name, I pray. Amen.

CHAPTER 9

THE LORD UNDERSTANDS OUR SUFFERING

❋ ❋ ❋

Dear Lord, who can relate to my
suffering better than you can? That's
why I come to you in prayer—because
I know that you understand what I'm
going through and because you know
the higher purpose my suffering serves.
I know that I can't see the light that
exists at the end of this long, dark
tunnel. But I also know that the light
is there and that you are with me as
I move closer to it each day. You know
my pain, and you know why I must
experience it. I have faith, Lord, that
all will be well and right in my world
soon. Amen.

❋ ❋ ❋

※ ※ ※

The reason why Christ chose the hard way of
the cross was, among other things,
that he saw beyond it.

—S. J. REID

※ ※ ※

When you were asked to suffer, Lord
Jesus, you did so without hesitation.
Your courage and your faith inspire
me to see my own suffering in a different light. I still do not like it nor wish
it to continue, but because of your
example, I can handle it with courage,
grace, and the knowledge that my
hardships are part of your plan for my
life. You did not back down in the face
of fear, and like you, I hope to find
the strength to face my fears, move

through them, and come out on the other side with a new sense of hope and possibility. Amen.

❋ ❋ ❋

"We can give our burdens to the Lord because he truly understands our pain."

❋ ❋ ❋

Dear Lord, you told your followers that they could cast their burdens upon you and that you would take their suffering away. I suffer now and ask that you take this burden from me and bring some relief from the pain and confusion that now fill my life. I know that I'm only so strong and that your strength can help me move past these difficult circumstances and see the goodness in my life again. Take my burden and let me cast my cares upon you, Lord. Help me carry on and get through. Amen.

※ ※ ※

[Jesus said,] "If any want to become my followers, let them deny themselves and take up their cross daily and follow me. For those who want to save their life will lose it, and those who lose their life for my sake will save it."

—LUKE 9:23–24

※ ※ ※

Heavenly Father, how can I come to you with my problems when there are so many people who are suffering far more than I am? I feel needy and selfish, but I don't know where to turn or how to deal with things the way they are. I ask in prayer that you show me some light upon which I can focus my heart and my hope—light that will lead me forward through the darkness knowing that on the other side of suffering there will be eternal joy. Lord, please hear my prayer.

※ ※ ※

No one is exempt from tragedy or disappointment—God himself was not exempt. Jesus offered no way out of the unfairness, but rather a way through it to the other side. Out of the darkness, a bright light shone.

—PHILIP YANCEY

※ ※ ※

Dear God, how blessed I am to have someone who understands the deepest part of me. No matter what I'm feeling or going through, you know my heart and all of its shadows. Your wisdom is always exactly what I need to hear and when I need to hear it, and your comfort shields me from the cold and the dark. I find hope and courage and a sense of purpose in you that keeps me going even when my days are filled with chaos and disorder. Thank you for truly understanding me.

❈ ❈ ❈

Father God, how your beloved Son, Jesus Christ, must have suffered for us! Yet here we are with our petty complaints about life, not realizing that we could have it much worse. Today I would like to pray for the inner peace that only you can give and for the well-being of others. I'm grateful to know that I can overcome anything with your love, God, but now I would like to assure others of that same love, which is available to them anytime they go to you and ask for it. May they be brought back home to you in faith.

※ ※ ※

Blessed are you when people hate you, and when they exclude you, revile you, and defame you on account of the Son of Man. Rejoice in that day and leap for joy, for surely your reward is great in heaven: for that is what their ancestors did to the prophets.

—LUKE 6:22–23

※ ※ ※

Lord God, I pray to you today for a little bit of grace in handling the challenges of my life. I've fought intolerance and impatience, and I've grown tired and angry more times than I care to think of. I long for happier, lighter times, but I know that first I must pass through these trials. I pray for grace, and some comfort, too, so that even as

I find the inner strength to face what must be faced, I will rest secure in the knowledge that I'm never alone. Thank you, Lord.

❈ ❈ ❈

"Just as the sufferings of Christ flow over into our lives, so also through Christ our comfort overflows to others."

❈ ❈ ❈

Dear God, you are my comforter and my protector, my refuge and my guide. I look to you for the light that serves to bring me safely home through the high and mighty waves and the great winds. You are the lighthouse upon the shore, and I watch for your light and follow where it leads: directly out of

suffering and back into happiness and
joy once again. I may always have
trials, but I know that I also will
always find my way out through your
guidance. You are my comforter and
my protector, my refuge and my guide.

※ ※ ※

*[His disciples] went and woke [Jesus] up, saying,
"Lord, save us! We are perishing!" And he said to
them, "Why are you afraid, you of little faith?"
Then he got up and rebuked the winds and the sea;
and there was a dead calm.*

—Matthew 8:25–26

※ ※ ※

Father God, you gave us your only
begotten Son so that we could learn
from his life and his example. I know
that suffering is a part of life and that

no one is immune, and I'm willing to endure my share of suffering. I only ask that you stand beside me to make sure that I can handle all that is given to me with grace, patience, and kindness. Often when my life is in shambles, I lash out at those closest to me. Help me be more like Jesus, who suffered terribly, yet still loved others with a selfless compassion.

❋ ❋ ❋

*He has raised up a mighty savior for us in the
house of his servant David, as he spoke through the
mouth of his holy prophets from of old, that we
would be saved from our enemies and from
the hand of all who hate us.*

—LUKE 1:69–71

❋ ❋ ❋

You chose to suffer for my benefit,
Lord Jesus, and I thank you with all
my heart. On the other hand, I know
that my suffering is for my own benefit
to help me grow and become a better
person. I know that you understand
my pain, and knowing that truly comforts me. Just to be heard and understood does a lot to make my troubles
worthwhile. Your loving presence

continues to provide me with the strength and fortitude I need to keep going down the path you set before me. And I thank you for helping me see the silver lining around each and every cloud.

❈ ❈ ❈

"No one understands my pain like Jesus, who suffered as one of us and came back to comfort us in our sorrows."

❈ ❈ ❈

O God, I can finally see some light at the end of this tunnel. The past few months have been so trying and so difficult, but now I feel my spirit lifting, and my heart is lighter, too. Thank you for being right here with me the

whole way, never leaving me even
when I complained too much or when
I was desperate and doubting. I could
not have made it this far without your
love, and now I'm looking forward
to this new lease on life that you have
given me. The suffering was worth
the joy of coming through it alive,
renewed, and filled with a sense of
release. Thank you, God.

※ ※ ※

It has been a long and trying time,
Lord, and I'm more than ready for
my burdens to be removed from
me. I pray that I can finally embrace
whatever lessons there are to be
learned and whatever wisdom there
is to be gleaned from this situation

in my heart and in my mind. I know that we all must have rain in our lives along with the sun, but how I miss the warmth of that sun on my face! I pray that this is the end of my dark nights for a while and that I can enjoy the light of a new day.

❋ ❋ ❋

Jesus knows the pain you feel. Take your burden to the Lord and leave it there.

—Charles Albert Tindley

❀ ❀ ❀

God, isn't there an easier way to grow
as a person? Suffering causes so much
pain, and when I'm going through it,
I often can't see the end of it. I know
that it must be for my own good, but
if possible, could you take some of this
weight off my shoulders? Just enough
so that I can continue onward and
upward. I pray for your help today.

❀ ❀ ❀

*I will show you what someone is like who comes to
me, hears my words, and acts on them. That one is
like a man building a house, who dug deeply and
laid the foundation on rock; when a flood arose,
the river burst against the house but could not
shake it, because it had been well built.*

—LUKE 6:47–48

❊ ❊ ❊

Here in my daily life, almighty God,
I endure hardships both small and
great, knowing that one day I will be
rewarded in heaven. Because your
Son suffered on earth and rejoiced in
heaven, I take heart knowing that I,
too, will rejoice in heaven after my
time to die has come. I hold strongly to
my faith, knowing that everything has
a season and a reason and that there
can't be light without dark or day
without night. This gives me peace,
even when everything around me is
disruptive and chaotic. I pray in Jesus'
precious name. Amen.

❊ ❊ ❊

O children of Zion, be glad and rejoice in the Lord your God; for he has given the early rain for your vindication, he has poured down for you abundant rain, the early and the later rain, as before. The threshing floors shall be full of grain, the vats shall overflow with wine and oil.

JOEL 2:23–24

※ ※ ※

Lord Jesus, you are my inspiration and my hope. In you I see what I want to be and how I want to walk through the world. You took your burdens and did not complain. You stood in the face of fear and did not let it overwhelm you. You held your ground and did not compromise your integrity and values, even when doing so might have saved you from suffering. I look to you

as a model of the kind of person I hope
to become. Mold and shape me into
your image, Lord. Amen.

※ ※ ※

Jesus shared our earthly life, and ascended
to prepare our heavenly life.

—"THE GELASIAN SACRAMENTARY"

※ ※ ※

Dear Lord, show me the way out of
my suffering. I'm not asking that you
take it away from me, only that you
show me how I can survive it with my
head and my heart intact. I know that
you suffered, and by your experience
and wisdom I hope to be able to rise to
my challenges and learn what you have
to teach me. I know this is a trial by
fire, and with you by my side I'm not

afraid of being burned...I only want
to be made righteous in Christ. Amen.

✼ ✼ ✼

*"Christ suffered for you so that you should follow
in his steps. Therefore, I have faith knowing God
feels and shares all my burdens and trials."*

❊ ❊ ❊

Is there a purpose to my misery, God?
Is there a point to my pain and suffering? I long to know the purpose. I
want to trust that your will is at work
here in my life. I suppose all I can do is
keep surrendering and letting it all go
so that you can best handle the situations that I cannot. But this takes a lot
of faith, God! So please deepen my
faith in you to do for me what might
seem impossible right now in the
midst of my hurt and anger. It's hard
to completely let go, but I'm doing that
now in prayer. Thank you, God, for
handling my problems and carrying
my burdens.

※ ※ ※

O God, it helps so much to know that whatever I'm feeling, you are feeling it too, and that whatever suffering I'm asked to deal with, you are dealing with it too. I feel as though I have a constant and loving parent watching over me at all times, looking out for me. Sensing your presence makes me feel stronger and more confident about my place in the world. Thank you for your presence and your power in my life. I recognize that you are always with me, even in the bad times, for it is then that my heart seeks you the most.

※ ※ ※

I will sing of your steadfast love, O Lord, forever; with my mouth I will proclaim your faithfulness to all generations. I declare that your steadfast love is established forever; your faithfulness is as firm as the heavens.

—PSALM 89:1–2

❖ ❖ ❖

When will I learn, Lord, that some temptations are best left alone? I know in my head that my suffering comes from giving into temptations, but my head isn't always in charge of my heart or my thoughts, it seems. Please help me have the inner strength and the integrity to avoid as much negative temptation as possible. And when I do give in and get hurt, help me have the faith and the courage to learn from my mistakes and accept responsibility for my actions. I may not be perfect, but I'm trying, Lord!

❋ ❋ ❋

"Jesus understands our every weakness because he was tempted in the same ways that we are tempted."

❋ ❋ ❋

Christ, help me have the same faith that you had when you were called upon to face your fears. Help me have the same strength that you had when you were called upon to resist temptation. Help me have the same courage you showed when dealing with those who wanted to do you harm. By your perfect example, I hope to live an exemplary life. With you as my inspiration, I hope to one day inspire others to follow the same path you have laid out for me. Lord, please help me be as

much like you as I humanly can. I pray
in your name. Amen.

❋ ❋ ❋

*Whoever does not carry the cross and follow me
cannot be my disciple. For which of you, intending
to build a tower, does not first sit down
and estimate the cost, to see whether he has
enough to complete it?*

—LUKE 14:27–28

※ ※ ※

Forgive me, God, for my weaknesses
and insecurities. Please shower me
with mercy and grace when I come up
short or fail to live up to your righteous standard. I pray to you today so
that I might know your presence more
deeply and make better decisions that
more accurately reflect your will for
my life. I may sometimes do the wrong
thing, but with your love and kindness
and compassion, I know that I can be
more obedient and do what is right. I
may not often act as mature as I would
like, but with your patience, I'm learn-
ing more and more each day. Thank
you, God, for your mercy, your grace,
your patience, and your forgiveness.

❈ ❈ ❈

Where there is suffering, Lord, let me be a beacon of hope for others. Where there is pain, let me somehow find a way to comfort those who can't comfort themselves. Where there is violence, let me be the calm that helps restore harmony. Where there is anguish, let me be a soothing balm. I have been blessed with good times and bad, and I know that the bad have been just as important to my growth as the good. So now, Lord, let me help others who have not yet come to understand your deep workings in their lives. Where there is confusion, let me be clarity. Use me, Lord, in any way you can today and every day of my life.

※ ※ ※

You have something eternally precious in common with Christ—suffering!

—JONI EARECKSON TADA AND STEVEN ESTES

※ ※ ※

Dear Father, sometimes I forget how blessed I am. I forget to be grateful. I forget to be patient. I forget to be kind. I forget that suffering is something we all must go through, and that our attitude determines how we come out of it. I ask that you help me slow down enough to see just how good life is, even when things appear to be not so good on the outside. Help me see the silver linings around each cloud. Life can be hard, but if I keep my eyes on you, it is worth every moment.

CHAPTER 10

THE LORD STRENGTHENS OUR FAITH

※ ※ ※

Dear heavenly Father, you have been
my helper, my comfort, my protector,
my provider—my everything—for
some time now. Because I have come
to trust in you, I can't imagine my life
without you. Over time, your faithfulness has steadied my faith in you. Your
goodness to me has softened my cyni-
cism. Your love has covered my faults.
Your salvation has given me a hope
and a future. Thank you for leading
me along this path of life.

※ ※ ※

*"Faith is the foundation upon which a happy,
healthy life is built. The stronger our faith, the
less our life can be shaken by outside occurrences
and extraneous circumstances."*

※ ※ ※

Whenever I've tried to do things my way, Lord, we've both seen the outcome. I have a long list of failed attempts at self-management. It's through these failures, however, that I've come to understand that your way is best. I don't have the perspective of seeing things from the beginning to the end as you do. And so, whenever I trust in you, listening to you speak to me from your Word and through your Holy Spirit, I don't have to worry about outcomes, because you always bring about what's best for me.

※ ※ ※

Trust in the Lord with all your heart, and do not rely on your own insight. In all your ways

acknowledge him, and he will make
straight your paths.

—PROVERBS 3:5–6

❋ ❋ ❋

I remember, almighty God, when
my level of trust in you was foolishly
small. I had many misconceptions
about you, and rumors about what
you were like hung in the back of my
mind. Were you out to punish me at
my first misstep? Are you always angry
and difficult to please? Since I placed
my life in your hands, was I doomed to
a dismal existence? Would you make
me suffer continually? I feel kind of
ashamed of those awful thoughts
now that I know the truth about you.
Thank you for your patience and love
that have gently led me into a fuller

understanding of your goodness and your faithfulness to my total welfare.

❋ ❋ ❋

Walking with you, dear Lord, has been such a series of pleasant surprises and gifts. It's not that there haven't been hard times, but those hard times would have come into my life anyway. It's your presence, Lord, that has made the difference. I believe I have experienced a multitude of blessings from your hand, but you also have been there with me in every trial, soothing my anguish with your compassion and giving me your strength, courage, and perspective. In good times and bad, you've taught me that I can always count on you being here with me.

※ ※ ※

This is a constant process in my life. God exchanging His presence for my loneliness—His power for my weakness—His healing for my illness—His hope for my despair—His peace for my anxiety—His love for my resentment— His grace for my suffering— His comfort for my sorrow.

—Evelyn Christenson

❋ ❋ ❋

It's always something! Life never quits handing out lemons, Lord. Sometimes I foolishly think that the current batch of lemons will hopefully be the last batch I'll get, but then there's the lemon truck pulling into my driveway again. Help me be able to smile whenever those lemons get delivered to my doorstep, knowing that you will show me what I need to do with them. You've helped me every time I've asked you, bringing good out of each bad situation. Thank you, Lord.

❋ ❋ ❋

Trust in the Lord, and do good; so you will live in the land, and enjoy security. Take delight in the Lord, and he will give you the desires of your heart.

—PSALM 37:3–4

❈ ❈ ❈

Dear heavenly Father, if I had to live my life according to the stock market or the weather, or how my favorite sports team is doing, I'd go crazy. If my happiness or well-being depended on those things, I'd be doomed. I'm so grateful that no matter what is going on around me—what circumstances are shifting under my feet—your grip on my life is firm, never compromised nor changed by anything this life dishes out. Indeed, you are my rock.

❈ ❈ ❈

"What a relief in this throwaway world of ever-changing values to know that God is the same yesterday, today, and tomorrow. He is as sure as a sunrise and a sunset."

❋ ❋ ❋

I used to fret, Lord, when people
had wrong impressions about me or
believed things that weren't true about
me. I used to think I had to set the
record straight as soon as possible. But
you've taught me that, more often than
not, it's best to wait and let truth win
its own victories over time. You have
a way of bringing the truth to light
in far better ways than I ever could.
So when justice seems far away, and
when unfairness and lies surround me,
remind me again, Lord, that you will
again, as you have done many times
before, declare the truth on my behalf.

❋ ❋ ❋

❈ ❈ ❈

Commit your way to the Lord; trust in him, and he will act. He will make your vindication shine like the light, and the justice of your cause like the noonday.

—Psalm 37:5–6

❈ ❈ ❈

My supreme God, I'm so grateful that I can confidently come to you with anything that is on my heart and mind. I know that you have said in your Word that I can cast *all* my cares on you, because you care for me, but I didn't always believe that my prayers could include things like the small details of my life or the negative feelings of anger and frustration I sometimes struggle with. Instead, you have taught me that you will always receive me when I come to you. Thank you for being such a compassionate God.

※ ※ ※

"There are many events in our lives over which we have no control. Our trust in God produces the endurance that sees us through the tough times we all face in this life."

※ ※ ※

Sadly, God, there have been some
foolish things I've trusted in the past!
I mean, things I've trusted in ways I
should only have trusted you for. I've
tried to make gods out of other people,
possessions, positions, and power. I
shudder to think of my foolishness
in putting these things in your place.
None of them have proved trustwor-
thy, faithful, or able to help me in
times of need, let alone able to love me
as you do! I know now that the place
reserved only for you in my life will
never have a rival. You alone are worthy of my trust and love.

※ ※ ※

❊ ❊ ❊

*There is none like you among the gods, O Lord, nor
are there any works like yours.... For you are great
and do wondrous things; you alone are God.*

—PSALM 86:8, 10

❊ ❊ ❊

As I recall the ways you've deepened
my faith, God, there are certain faces
that come to mind—people you put in
my path—people who have a remark-
able faith stemming from a vibrant
relationship with you. How these
people have shaped my understanding
of your love and faithfulness! Thank
you for each one, for their prayers, for
their transparency, for their kindness,
and also for their patience with me.
I have seen what you are like through

them. How blessed I am to have, or have had, each one in my life!

※ ※ ※

"As we learn to trust God, we discover his strengthening presence in various places and in different people. Whenever we find shelter, comfort, rest, and peace, we are bound to hear his voice, welcoming us."

⁂ ⁂ ⁂

The streams of my heart used to flow in so many different directions, searching for pools of loyalty and love. How often they were emptied into desert sands or stinky swamplands! Disappointment and disillusionment are the bitter pills of youth. But then I encountered the ocean of your love and faithfulness, Lord. What a difference you have made in my life! My whole heart runs as one river now toward you and you alone.

⁂ ⁂ ⁂

Teach me your way, O Lord, that I may walk in your truth; give me an undivided heart to revere your name.

—Psalm 86:11

❋ ❋ ❋

Thank you for the promises in your
Word, Lord, that sustain my faith
when the stretch of life's road I'm on
seems to pass through a wasteland.
As I'm trudging forward, I recall what
you have said in the Scriptures, and
I'm able to press on. I repeat those
lines of vital assurance, and my hope
revives. I've learned to cling to your
Word when there is nothing else in
sight, because I know you do not lie
and you will keep every promise you
have ever made.

❋ ❋ ❋

A mighty fortress is our God,
a bulwark never failing.

—MARTIN LUTHER

✵ ✵ ✵

Depression is such a deep pit of the soul, Father in heaven. You have carried me out of that pit more than once, and each time you stayed with me the entire time. Where others could not reach me, you took a hold of me. When others could not understand, you listened and consoled me. While others offered their best advice to no avail, you spoke words of life and healing to me. This is one of many reasons I will never stop praising you, holy Father. How perfect your wisdom is! How great is your steadfast love! You have taught me to trust you, even in the darkest nights of the soul.

✵ ✵ ✵

※ ※ ※

I give thanks to you, O Lord my God, with my whole heart, and I will glorify your name forever. For great is your steadfast love toward me; you have delivered my soul from the depths of Sheol.

—Psalm 86:12–13

※ ※ ※

I like to recall the ways you have shown your faithfulness to me over time, Lord. I like to think back through the decades and remember the highlights of your steadfast love. There have been the miracles—great and small—of provision, protection, and healing. There have been the divine appointments with people whom you have given me the privilege of helping, and those who have helped

me, as well. There have been the timely
blessings and encouragements and the
gifts of life and love. Since there is so
much evidence of your faithfulness to
me, I really do have to narrow it down
to the highlights. You've blessed me
beyond measure!

※ ※ ※

"Ah, what solace there is in God's promise of
peace! True help and real peace are to be found
in trusting in his guidance and inspiration."

※ ※ ※

When I lift up faith like a shield in my
life, Lord God, when I raise my trust
in you at the first sign of trouble, how
changed my perspective becomes! I
see you standing between me and my

challenges; I see you making a way for
me to victory; I see your strength and
your wisdom coming to my aid. My
knees stop knocking together, and my
heart is filled with courage. May a
song of victorious praise be on my lips
today, Lord, as I hold high this faith
you have caused to live within me.

❋ ❋ ❋

*Stand therefore, and fasten the belt of truth around
your waist, and put on the breastplate of
righteousness. As shoes for your feet put on whatever
will make you ready to proclaim the gospel of peace.
With all of these, take the shield of faith,
with which you will be able to deflect all
the flaming arrows of the evil one.*

—Ephesians 6:14–16

※ ※ ※

Even when my faith fails, dear God, your love does not. Thank you for holding on to me through thick and thin. When I've felt too weak to hold on to you and have believed that all would be lost in the storm, I've discovered that you always keep me safe in your loving arms. Sheltered and cradled there, I am reassured that nothing can separate me from your love. It's this amazing love of yours that I have come to trust so gratefully.

❈ ❈ ❈

"God's love is wider than our worries, longer than our loneliness, stronger than our sorrows, deeper than our doubts, and higher than our hostilities. Just as valleys are wide, rivers are long, winds are strong, oceans are deep, and the sky is high, so we can have a picture of the wonder of God's love."

❈ ❈ ❈

Each day as I walk alongside you, Lord, I learn more about trusting you and about living in this faith you have established in my heart. I pray that these roots of trust will grow strong, deep, and wide and that loving obedience to your voice will flourish as a result. Thank you for speaking to my heart through your Word and by your Spirit, who leads me into all truth. I love this journey of faith: What an adventure! And what a blessing!

❈ ❈ ❈

As you therefore have received Christ Jesus the Lord, continue to live your lives in him, rooted and built up in him and established in the faith, just as you were taught, abounding in thanksgiving.

—Colossians 2:6–7

❈ ❈ ❈

It's much easier now to walk in faith than it used to be, heavenly Father. How I used to worry, wondering if you'd come through! Now I just wait for you, knowing it's not a matter of *if* but *when* your answer or intervention will come. And I have learned, too, that your timing is flawless. You are never too late, never too early, always on time. And so now, even while everything may look like chaos on the outside, I can be calm on the inside. I can sleep at night and go peacefully through my day because I know you are in control.

❈ ❈ ❈

Lord, you reveal many pictures of your love for me in the Scriptures. Today I recall the metaphor of a hen gathering her tiny chicks under her wings for protection and warmth, just as you gather those who belong to you under the shelter of your love. My soul can know the contentment of that place of refuge today as I come to you in faith. I hide there, trusting that you care for me and will keep me safely tucked away within the blessing of your tender mercies.

❋ ❋ ❋

"I'm grateful to the Lord for reaching out and drawing me under his wings. His love is so great that he knows my troubles, is concerned for my welfare, and is working to renew my joy."

❋ ❋ ❋

The tests of time have strengthened and purified my faith in you, Lord. You have purged away the conditions I used to put on you—all those "Lord, I'll trust you if…" prayers. You've smelted away the doubt that used to set up contingency plans in case you didn't come through for me. You've done away with my reliance on my own understanding for approaching life's challenges. How different my faith looks today because you have patiently and faithfully refined it in your wisdom and love!

❖ ❖ ❖

In this you rejoice, even if now for a little while you have had to suffer various trials, so that the genuineness of your faith—being more precious than gold that, though perishable, is tested by fire—may be found to result in praise and glory and honor when Jesus Christ is revealed.

—1 Peter 1:6–7

❈ ❈ ❈

God, not everyone understands and appreciates my faith in you. People sometimes see my waiting on you as passiveness. At other times, they see my boldness in moving forward into the unseen truth of your promises as foolishness. Faith is often the opposite of what a person would naturally be inclined to do, so I understand why they wonder about me. I know it looks funny or strange from the outside, but when your guidance is clear to me on the inside, I can't worry about what others will think. Though I shun public opinion as a means of navigating my life, I pray that you would reveal yourself to those who do not know you yet. May they see the wisdom of your ways as the fruit of my faith ripens before their eyes.

❊ ❊ ❊

I'm here, Father, because you have been faithful to me. It is your faithfulness that has initiated, nurtured, and strengthened my faith in you. I can't imagine life without you now. It would be no life at all, as far as I can tell. And though you are unseen, you are more real to me than any mortal whose face I can see and touch. My hope is that this faith you have planted within me will always remain and will never be uprooted by any event or circumstance life may bring. Please keep me close to you so that one day I may stand before you in your glory.

❋ ❋ ❋

It is grace that brought me safe thus far,
and grace will lead me home.

—John Newton

❋ ❋ ❋

I want the young people in my life to
learn to trust in you, Lord, as you have
taught me to do. I pray for them today.
I ask that you would reveal yourself
to them in ways they can perceive and
respond to. I pray that you will find
them at times and in places where
peer pressure is not tugging at them
and when they can stop and listen and
know that you are speaking to them,
calling to them, and drawing them
near. Challenge their faithlessness with
your truth and love. Illuminate the

reality of life's emptiness without you.
May they hunger and thirst for you
and find you to be exactly what they
have been longing for.

❀ ❀ ❀

I will sing of your steadfast love, O Lord, forever;
with my mouth I will proclaim your faithfulness
to all generations. I declare that your steadfast
love is established forever; your faithfulness
is as firm as the heavens.

—Psalm 89:1–2

❀ ❀ ❀

Dear Lord, there are those who think
there cannot be a God because of the
evil in the world. It truly makes me
sad that they cannot see the manifold
blessings of your benevolence despite
the reality of a fallen world. It deeply

pains my heart that they cannot trust that you have an ultimate plan for dealing with evil and that you have prepared a way of salvation for anyone who would receive it. How heart-rending it is to know that you extend your love and goodness to them but they cannot perceive it! O Father, help those who desire to have faith but cannot find their way to it. In Jesus' name, I pray. Amen.

CHAPTER 11

GOD ALWAYS KEEPS HIS PROMISES

❊ ❊ ❊

O God, there are times when I feel as
if I don't have a friend in the world—
no one who really cares about me or
what I'm going through. Everyone I
know seems to be too busy with their
own lives and their own problems. But
I'm so grateful that you are always here
with me no matter how often I need
you. Your promise of eternal love is my
bedrock of strength that helps me get
through the challenges of my life, even
when those who love me don't have
the time or patience to help. Thank
you, God, for never abandoning me.

❊ ❊ ❊

*"We know that there are few greater
disappointments than to think no one cares or*

understands. That is why Jesus' promise of his eternal presence is truly precious to us, for he promised, 'Remember, I am with you always, to the end of the age.' "

❀ ❀ ❀

Dear Lord, I pray for release from the pain and suffering I'm going through. I know that you are here with me, watching over me, and that you will never give me something I'm not equipped to handle. I know that I can lean on you when I'm weak and tired and without strength. But I still ask for some relief from my struggles and release from the pain. I put my faith and hope in you to keep the promises you made to me. Lord, please stay with me and don't give up on me.

※ ※ ※

Heavenly Father, how good it is to
know that you understand me, even
when others don't! I don't have to
explain myself to you, because you
know my mind, my heart, and my
soul. Just having you in my life makes
me feel as though I have a companion
to walk beside me through sunny fields
and dark valleys, a companion who
won't run off and leave me at the first
sign of trouble. Your steadfast love is
what keeps me strong. How good it is
to know you are always with me!

※ ※ ※

In the beginning, Lord, you founded the earth, and
the heavens are the work of your hands; they will
perish, but you remain; they will all wear out like

clothing; like a cloak you will roll them up,
and like clothing they will be changed.

—HEBREWS 1:10–12

❋ ❋ ❋

It took me a long time to get here, Lord—to a place where I have total faith in you. I fought and resisted you every step of the way, but when I finally realized that you never failed to keep the promises you made to me, I also realized that you would never harm or abandon me. My faith in you has become my fortress and my freedom, for I know that I don't have to fight and resist you any longer. I can enjoy my life and relax in the understanding that no matter what happens, you are here with me. Amen.

※ ※ ※

"Faithfulness comes from a God who has kept and is in the process of fulfilling every promise revealed in Scriptures. We are commanded to have faith in God, and out of that faith flows our ability to keep the promises we have made as husbands and wives, as children, as parents, and as servants of God."

※ ※ ※

As your beloved child, Father in heaven, I place my hope and my faith entirely in you and your will for my life. In the Scriptures, I'm told that your love for me never ends, even upon death. And so, I surrender to your will and your guidance, knowing that as I continue to serve you, I will continue to be blessed with your loving presence. My faith in you helps me have faith in myself, and in others, too. Blessings abound, Father, when I place my hope and my faith entirely in you!

※ ※ ※

My brothers and sisters, whenever you face trials of any kind, consider it nothing but joy, because you know that the testing of your faith produces

endurance; and let endurance have its full effect,
so that you may be mature and
complete, lacking in nothing.

—James 1:2–4

❈ ❈ ❈

Sometimes I get the feeling, God, that I'm all alone in this world. Things go wrong, and I can't find the right solutions. People react in ways I can't control or predict. I just feel as though there's no point or purpose to it all. Please help me find a deeper truth about life, a truth that will get me through the confusing and frustrating times when nothing seems to go my way. Help me understand that it all happens for a reason and that the reason is your will for me. I know your

will is the promise of a better life; I
just need your help to remain steadfast
in my faith in you.

❋ ❋ ❋

*Likewise all to whom God gives wealth and
possessions and whom he enables to enjoy them,
and to accept their lot and find enjoyment in their
toil—this is the gift of God. For they will scarcely
brood over the days of their lives, because God keeps
them occupied with the joys of their hearts.*

—ECCLESIASTES 5:19–20

❋ ❋ ❋

Which way do I go, Lord? What
choice do I make? I'm told in the Bible
that your thoughts are higher than my
thoughts and that your will is greater
than my will. I come to you in prayer
for signs of the direction you wish me

to take and the choices you wish me to make. Your promises of everlasting love and life give me faith and hope, but it's the guidance I often seem to lack. Help me focus on the little signs you give me each day, so that my path takes me to that higher place you have promised me. Thank you, Lord, for answering my prayer.

❖ ❖ ❖

Our confidence in the power of prayer is rooted in the promise that God is continually working for good in the midst of ambiguous situations and that God's purpose will prevail in the end.

—MARJORIE J. THOMPSON

❖ ❖ ❖

Dear Lord, you never fail to amaze me with the miracles you bless me with each day. I'm not talking about big, spectacular miracles, but those little things that remind me you care about me. My family, my friends, my work, the beautiful things I own—they are all reminders of your love for me, your cherished child. But even if I had no material possessions, Lord, I would still know that you loved me, because you gave me life, as well as the fulfillment of a promise to always walk with me throughout my life. I'm blessed and loved, and that is all I need to feel joy in my heart and happiness in my soul.

❈ ❈ ❈

You know in your hearts and souls, all of you, that not one thing has failed of all the good things that the Lord your God promised concerning you; all have come to pass for you, not one of them has failed.

—Joshua 23:14

❈ ❈ ❈

Dear Lord, I know there is bad and evil in this world. I see it all around me on the news and in my own life. But that does not stop me from clinging fast to my faith in you and to my hope that there is a place beyond this life where evil does not exist. I trust in your promises of heaven and of eternal love, and I know that if I keep my hope alive, I will one day see that

promise fulfilled. It does get hard,
when pain and suffering are so close
at hand, but your presence is the light
of hope that guides me through the
darkest of dark days. Thank you, Lord.

❊ ❊ ❊

*"Choosing to live as a people of hope is not to
diminish or belittle pain and suffering or to
ignore evil's reality. Instead, we cling to God's
promise that he will make all things new."*

❊ ❊ ❊

O God, your promise to make all
things new is what I need right now.
There seems to be so much old stuff
clogging up my life and making my
progress difficult if not impossible. I
know that a snake must shed its skin

now and then, and though I'm not a snake, it feels as if I can't get the old skin off and let the new skin out. Will you help me have the patience and the faith that all of these blocks will be removed one day and that the old will indeed give way to the new? I look forward with joyful expectation of those new days ahead, but I just wish they would come a little faster, God.

※ ※ ※

In the middle of the night, when all is
dark and frightening, the only thing I
have to hold onto, precious Lord, is the
promise of the coming dawn. When
my life is like the long, dark night, I
hold onto you and your love. I know
that if I can just make it through
the hours before daybreak, I will be
rewarded with the joy and warmth
that a new sunrise can bring. As these
long hours of night pass slowly by and
I wait for the first light of morning,
help me hold fast to you, Lord, as my
hope and salvation.

※ ※ ※

*[Jesus prayed,] "Now my soul is troubled. And
what should I say— 'Father, save me from this*

hour?' No, it is for this reason that I have come to this hour. Father, glorify your name."

—JOHN 12:27–28

❋ ❋ ❋

Today is a day for celebration, God, for all the wonderful gifts you have given me through your love and faith in me. The promise of your constant presence is a reason for singing out in joy and praise and in gratitude for blessings big and small. No matter what the new day ahead of me might bring, I know I'm not alone in this thing called life. You are here, ready to take up my cause at any time, and you are always on standby should I need you. Thank you, God, for being here with me and for never failing to fulfill your promises to me.

❈ ❈ ❈

"God's love is true and is always reaching out to us. His faithful love is cause for celebration."

❈ ❈ ❈

There are no sure things in life and no guarantees of happiness and joy, except when I turn to you, O God, for you alone are a sure thing and a guarantee of a life filled with love and peace and the kind of confidence that goes far beyond my outer achievements. With you, God, there may still be sad days to experience, but having you here beside me, urging me to carry on through the pain, makes me understand that there is a reason, a purpose, and a time for all things under heaven. You alone are my sure thing, God.

❋ ❋ ❋

The Lord is your keeper; the Lord is your shade at your right hand. The sun shall not strike you by day, nor the moon by night. The Lord will keep you from all evil; he will keep your life. The Lord will keep your going out and your coming in from this time on and forevermore.

—PSALM 121:5–8

❋ ❋ ❋

Lord Jesus, you suffered, so I could benefit from your pain, your experience, and your devotion to God. No matter how much you feared your destiny, you walked toward it with courage and the understanding that God would fulfill his promises to you. Now, help me do the same by overcoming my fears while knowing that the fulfillment of your promises to me lies waiting around the bend. I may not see the path ahead of me, but I can still step out in faith knowing with a full heart that you are walking beside me, ready to hold me up if I should stumble and fall. That was your promise to me, and I'm deeply grateful, Lord. Amen.

❋ ❋ ❋

"Faith is more than believing in who God is. It's believing that he will keep his promises."

❈ ❈ ❈

My friends tell me I have to have faith and "let go and let God," and yet when I try to let go, I feel resistance within me. It has always been hard for me to trust anyone, and yet I'm alive and well and that should be enough for me to trust in you, God. I pray today for a stronger faith and for the courage to give up control of my life to you. I pray for the ability to just surrender it all and let your Holy Spirit move me, instead of me always trying to figure it all out for myself. Help me have faith in you, God, and in your will for me.

❈ ❈ ❈

The prayer of faith will save the sick, and the Lord will raise them up; and anyone who has committed sins will be forgiven. Therefore confess your sins to one another, and pray for one another, so that you may be healed.

—JAMES 5:15–16

※ ※ ※

Lord, please take away my anxieties and my worries about tomorrow, and please let me rest awhile in the present moment. I spend so much time either regretting the past or completely stressing out over what might happen tomorrow that I forget the gift of the present and the awareness of your presence in my life. Only in the quiet and calm of the moment at hand can I sense that you are with me. Sometimes I forget you in the busyness of my life, and that is when my anxiety

returns. Help me, Lord, to stay in the
present and in that wonderful place of
peace and calm where I can listen to
your voice.

❊ ❊ ❊

Heavenly Father, give me the peace
that passes all understanding, a peace
so deep that no matter what storms
blow into my life I stand secure upon
the foundation of my faith in you.
Give me a peace that accompanies me
along even the scariest roads of life,
telling me that I have all the courage
and strength I need to handle anything
that crosses my path. Give me a peace
that soothes my heart when it is broken and calms my spirit when it is out
of harmony and balance. Give me your

peace, dear Father, for that is all I need. Amen.

※ ※ ※

Let us know the truth of His promise:
that the whole world may not be able
to take away His peace.

—Søren Kierkegaard

※ ※ ※

Dear Jesus, your promise of mercy and grace is cause for rejoicing. I long to show others just how much you have done for me and how your promises of eternal life and love have lifted me up from the dark places in my life. May I be a vessel of your love, pouring it out to others, and may I proclaim your good words and deeds so that those I come in contact with can see how

much you have transformed my life.
I want to celebrate this special relationship I have with you.

※ ※ ※

Therefore, since we are justified by faith, we have
peace with God through our Lord Jesus Christ,
through whom we have obtained access to this grace
in which we stand; and we boast in our hope
of sharing the glory of God.

—Romans 5:1–2

❈ ❈ ❈

It is one thing, O God, to tell the people in my life about all the wondrous miracles you've performed for me. But when they see the light in my eyes and feel the uplifting joy of my spirit, those things speak far more than words ever could. Your promise of unceasing love and concern for me shines through me like a beacon, attracting others to me. They want to know my secret of happiness, and I tell them there is no secret but you, dear God, at work in my life in the most mysterious of ways. May I be your light in the world to all who may need a way out of darkness.

❈ ❈ ❈

❋ ❋ ❋

Father in heaven, show me the light at
the end of this tunnel, because right
now the darkness of my pain and
suffering blinds me. I want so badly to
be happy and at peace again, but right
at this moment, it seems as though
that day will never arrive. Help me be
patient, courageous, and strong. Help
me keep focused on the road ahead,
and lead me back, step by step, into
the light of day. Help me have faith
that my suffering is for a reason and
that it will, indeed, come to an end.

❋ ❋ ❋

"In the midst of my sorrow, I cried great tears of
joy because of his priceless promise that he never
wastes our pain. On the other side of this trial,

I know for certain that I will see his purpose fulfilled, and as always, I will find reasons to celebrate."

❈ ❈ ❈

God, I know that most of my prayers ask for your help, and rarely do I take the time to stop and thank you for your help. I want to take that time right now and tell you that I'm forever grateful for the answers to my prayers you never fail to provide. I get so involved in life that I forget that you are continuously helping me be a better person. I thank you for molding my character and for all the blessings you have bestowed upon me, and even teaching me those hard lessons I complain about the most.

❊ ❊ ❊

Three times I appealed to the Lord about this [thorn in the flesh], that it would leave me, but he said to me, "My grace is sufficient for you, for power is made perfect in weakness." So, I will boast all the more gladly of my weaknesses, so that the power of Christ may dwell in me.

—2 CORINTHIANS 12:8–9

❊ ❊ ❊

My trials are many, Lord God, and my faith grows weak. I pray today for a stronger faith in your will and your purpose. I surrender to the timing of your grace, knowing that it may not arrive when I want it to, but it will arrive when I need it to. I ask for continued guidance and wisdom, dear Lord, so that I can overcome these trials to the best of my ability. I ask for your mercy so that these trials may never become anything I can't handle. Most of all, I ask that you remain beside me as my companion, my inspiration, and my friend.

❋ ❋ ❋

Dear Jesus, I'm putting my faith and hope in you, because I'm just not capable of doing any more than I've already done. I've exhausted every option, and now I want to cast all my burdens upon you, because you have promised to heal me and fill me with hope. Please take these burdens from me, so you can renew my strength and courage. Help me over the bridge between my suffering and

my happiness. Thank you for hearing
my prayer, Lord. Amen.

※ ※ ※

When outward strength is broken, faith rests on
the promises. In the midst of sorrow, faith draws
the sting out of every trouble, and takes out
the bitterness from every affliction.

—ROBERT CECIL

※ ※ ※

Dear Lord, in this day and age it has
become so easy to break our promises
to one another, but no matter how
busy or crazy my life gets, I try not
to break my promise to love you and
to love others. I know that if I live
according to your laws, I will be
rewarded with eternal joy beside you
in heaven. Though I may fail and even

sin at times, you always pick me up so
I can try to do what is right and be a
better person. You keep my hopes
alive, and I have my eyes on the prize
of the fulfillment of your heavenly
promises. In Jesus' name, I pray. Amen.

❈ ❈ ❈

*Be patient, therefore, beloved, until the coming of the
Lord. The farmer waits for the precious crop from
the earth, being patient with it until it receives the
early and late rains. You also must be patient.
Strengthen your hearts, for the coming
of the Lord is near.*

—JAMES 5:7–8

CHAPTER 12

THE LORD
CARES
FOR US

※ ※ ※

Sometimes, heavenly Father, I hear people talk about your love as if it were a consolation prize, a last resort, or a lackluster alternative to human love and acceptance. Oh, what a mistaken perspective we sometimes have of your tremendous love for us! Your love is deep and unshakable, faithful and far-reaching. It picks us up out of the depths when we are at our worst and then flings wide the door of acceptance when we return home to you. Your love is here when everyone else has gone away, and it waits for us when we wander off after fickle and false loves. Your love is the best prize among all prizes, and I value it above all other things.

※ ※ ※

For I am convinced that neither death, nor life, nor angels, nor rulers, nor things present, nor things to come, nor powers, nor height, nor depth, nor anything else in all creation, will be able to separate us from the love of God in Christ Jesus our Lord.

—ROMANS 8:38–39

※ ※ ※

It's a strange reality, Lord Jesus, the connection between suffering and love. When we needed to be rescued from evil, you endured great suffering for our sakes, and when we needed to be cleansed from our sins, you died so that we could become pure before God—and you did all this because you loved us so deeply. Mothers suffer through childbirth because of a powerful maternal love. Fathers sacrifice themselves in service to their families, sometimes working multiple jobs to provide shelter, food, and clothing for their family because of love. Remind me today, Lord, that my suffering doesn't have to be meaningless. I can offer it up to you, drawing near to your love, becoming more loving and compassionate toward others who suffer, and sharing in the fellowship of your sufferings.

❈ ❈ ❈

"How deep will the pain go? Rest assured, never deeper than the Lord's love."

❋ ❋ ❋

I think our culture often makes a
caricature of love, heavenly Father. We
think of love in terms of hearts and
teddy bears, chocolates and flowers,
romances and Norman Rockwell
moments. But when I look at your
best expression of love—your Son,
Jesus—my common notions of love
are swept away. In him, I see the
Wonderful Counselor speaking truth,
whether it was good news or uncom-
fortable realities. I see the Mighty God
walking in gentle humility, stooping to
serve us. I see the Everlasting Father
reaching down in empathy to offer
salvation to a stubbornly self-sufficient
humanity. And I see the Prince of
Peace entering our chaos and offering

his own self to bring the peace our souls so desperately need. Please fill my heart and mind with this kind of love, Father.

❊ ❊ ❊

Pride is the culprit behind my sinful ways, Lord. In my prideful moments, I think I know better than you do, or I think I can give truth the slip and make something work that I know isn't right. But these are foolish thoughts and ways! Wrong can never be right, and your wisdom is perfect. Please forgive me for my arrogance, Lord, in trying to do things my own way and in defying your way of truth and righteousness. Thank you for holding me to the truth and for faith-

fully correcting me and loving me
enough to discipline me. Thank you
for your "tough love."

❊ ❊ ❊

*I know, O Lord, that your judgments are right, and
that in faithfulness you have humbled me. Let your
steadfast love become my comfort according to
your promise to your servant.*

—PSALM 119:75–76

❊ ❊ ❊

I like to ponder your creation, my
Creator God, to wonder at its beauty
and complexity. I like to be outdoors
and let my senses take in the world
you have made. I like to watch and
listen to nature programs and learn
new things about the wonders of your
workmanship. Your Word tells me that

you made them in wisdom. There is no doubt! I also believe you made them in love, revealing yourself—your goodness, faithfulness, wisdom, and power—to all humanity. Thank you for these sacred gifts. I truly cherish each one of them.

※ ※ ※

Morning reminds me, Lord, that the darkness of night is temporary. Sunrise proclaims the promise that there is a dawning of salvation from each sorrow and each pain for those who trust in you. Whether or not we experience that dawning in this life, we know there is an ultimate dawning of eternal freedom from all suffering and sorrow when the line you have drawn on the horizon of time is made bright at your appearing.

※ ※ ※

How long must I bear pain in my soul, and have sorrow in my heart all day long?... But I trusted in your steadfast love; my heart shall rejoice in your salvation. I will sing to the Lord, because he has dealt bountifully with me.

—PSALM 13:2, 56

❋ ❋ ❋

Your love is an anchor for my soul,
Lord Jesus. The assurance that you
love me gives me a focus when nothing
seems to make any sense. It calms me
when I fear the worst. It keeps me
from despairing when I feel like a
failure. In every circumstance, I need
only recall the reality of your unfailing
love, and that is more than enough to
hold me steady and give me the peace
I need. Thank you, Jesus.

❋ ❋ ❋

I still struggle and do not expect to find all the
answers to the multitude of questions which
perplex my soul. My certainties have been few;
my doubts have been many. Yet the bedrock
assurance which has held my feet from slipping is

the confidence that God loves me and nothing occurs outside of His providential control.

—James E. Means

❋ ❋ ❋

Dear Lord, I think of how you have helped me so many times and in so many ways—how consistently you've loved me and brought me through hardships. I could write a book about it! And then, as if saving me is not enough, you bless me with good things. Your love gifts come in countless forms, and I know I take them for granted too often. But that doesn't seem to stop you from graciously giving them anyway. I just wanted to "notice" the blessings of your love in my life today. I want to give you praise for your steadfast love.

※ ※ ※

*I will exult and rejoice in your steadfast love,
because you have seen my affliction; you have taken
heed of my adversities, and have not delivered
me into the hand of the enemy; you have set
my feet in a broad place.*

—Psalm 31:7–8

※ ※ ※

Let each wreath, heavenly Father, be
a reminder of your perfect love for me.
Let the circle remind me that your
love has no beginning or end. Let the
evergreen boughs remind me that you
came to give me eternal life. Let the
red ribbon put me in mind of the gift
of your Son and his sacrifice. Let the
pine cones remind me to spread the
seed of your love by proclaiming the
gospel of your salvation. Thank you,
Father, for this meaningful way to
remember your faithful love during
the Christmas season.

※ ※ ※

For God so loved the world that he gave his only
Son, so that everyone who believes in him may not

perish but may have eternal life. Indeed, God did not send the Son into the world to condemn the world, but in order that the world might be saved through him.

—JOHN 3:16–17

※ ※ ※

For just a moment, Lord Jesus, I want to pull away from the hubbub of Christmas and send you a Valentine message. I love you. I truly do. And I can love you because you first loved me. Without your love, I would not have learned what true love is. So I just wanted to say thank you for loving me first and for showing me how to love you back. It never gets old—your love for me—and I never get tired of telling you how much your love means to me. You are the love of my life.

❈ ❈ ❈

God, how I enjoy sitting in a darkened
room with no lights on except for the
Christmas tree lights. Whether silence
prevails or Christmas hymns play
softly, I feel a sense of reverent peace
as I worship you. In those sacred
moments, I bring my heart to you,
offering my grateful homage in
response to your amazing love. How
I long to remain near to you as the
season moves toward its crescendo!
Hold me in this place of peace within,
no matter what's transpiring without.

❈ ❈ ❈

*"Beneath the supporting hands of friends
and helpers, we feel God's strong grasp,
and we hold on, no longer alone."*

✵ ✵ ✵

Do you never tire of my coming to you, Lord God? Don't you grow weary when I always have another thing to ask? Do you really not mind my always pondering things in your presence? I get tired of myself sometimes, so it seems incredible that you would continually welcome me without wanting a break from my company. But I'm glad your invitation remains open to me. Your love is beyond comprehension. It stands in stark contrast to my human limitations and failings when it comes to relationships and loving other people. So please help me to learn from your love, to grow in it, and then to pass it on to others. Thank you, Lord, for your continuous presence in my life! I pray with an open heart. Amen.

※ ※ ※

Lord Jesus, you knew we'd never be able to merit your grace. And so, in love, you took the initiative to save us. Thank you for your proactive love that doesn't wait to receive before it gives. Thank you for your zealous love that charges forward into our apathy and self-centeredness. Thank you for your steadfast love that just doesn't give up. Thank you for loving me with such a great love as you revealed on the cross.

❈ ❈ ❈

For while we were still weak, at the right time Christ died for the ungodly. Indeed, rarely will anyone die for a righteous person—though perhaps for a good person someone might actually dare to die. But God proves his love for us in that while we still were sinners Christ died for us.

—Romans 5:6–8

❈ ❈ ❈

I can run from your love, heavenly Father, and I may even succeed in rejecting it for a time, but you will never stop offering it to me. I think of the prodigal's father, who waited and watched in hope for the safe return of his wayward son. You are that Father who never withdraws his love, no matter the insult or injury to himself.

Yours is the noblest of loves, a self-sacrificing love, a beautiful love to behold, and the best love to be held by.

※ ※ ※

"In this world where human love is conditional and often temporary, it is a joy to know that God loves us unconditionally and eternally. Nothing we can say or do will cause God to stop loving us."

※ ※ ※

The changing seasons, my Creator, remind me of your faithful love. For countless generations, these yearly cycles have cued our planting, growing, harvesting, and resting. In your wisdom, you've made a proper time for everything. In your love, you have

created us to understand and enjoy
your design in the seasonal variations.
How blessed I feel to live in your
amazing world and to see your love
displayed in its wonders!

✵ ✵ ✵

The Lord takes pleasure in those who fear him, in
those who hope in his steadfast love.... He gives
snow like wool; he scatters frost like ashes....
He sends out his word, and melts them; he
makes his wind blow, and the waters
flow.... Praise the Lord!

—Psalm 147:11, 16, 18, 20

✵ ✵ ✵

Your love does not spare me from
every difficulty, Lord, but in your love,
you are with me through each difficult
thing I face and with each step I take.

Your love does not make my pain nonexistent in this life, but your love sustains me as I go through the pain. And with each hardship you carry me through, you remind me of your promise of a future in which none of these trials will find me ever again. Lord, I trust your love enough to know that this hope is sure and that my future with you in paradise is secure.

✵ ✵ ✵

"May you be assured of God's presence as you weather this current storm. As the waves toss you about, and the ship of your life threatens to crash into rough rocks: He is there. Never despair. After all, he created all these things, and in him alone they have their existence."

✵ ✵ ✵

My affections come and go; sometimes I'm more loving, sometimes less. But your love, dear God, is steadfast. Your Word says that your love for me never ceases and that your mercies for me are renewed each morning. I don't deserve your abundance of love and mercy, but you give it to me freely and willingly. Truly, I receive your love gratefully. Only let me not stop there;

help me offer that kind of steadfast love to those around me, whether they deserve it or not. Let your love flow through me so that there will be a continuity of true loving kindness at work in my life, ministering to others, regardless of my mood or circumstances.

Heavenly Father, please forgive me for expecting others to love me perfectly. (Truly, only you can love me that way.) Indeed, at times I fail to love others as I should. Help me let others off the hook when their love lets me down. Please grant me a heart to forgive, just as you have forgiven me. I don't want old hurts and grudges—or new ones, for that matter—to stand in the way of a truly blessed Christmas celebration. Instead, I pray that the reality of imperfect human love would remind me of why I need your love so much.

✳ ✳ ✳

"You've never been so loved by man, woman, or child as by God. Indeed, the Lord gave his very best—his Son—so you could become one of his children."

❋ ❋ ❋

Anticipation is delightful now that I've become an adult, Lord. And yet, I remember how painful it was when I was a child at Christmas time. Oh, the agony of waiting to find out what was in that package with my name on it! It reminds me of how anxious I used to be waiting for your answers, waiting for you to come through for me, and waiting to see if you'd really help me. Thankfully, it's different now. Waiting is not the hand-wringing trial it used to be. Now I can relax even while outcomes are unknown to me because I know that you love me, that you are with me, and that you have my life under control.

❈ ❈ ❈

I pray that you may have the power to comprehend, with all the saints, what is the breadth and length and height and depth, and to know the love of Christ that surpasses knowledge, so that you may be filled with all the fullness of God.

—Ephesians 3:18–19

❈ ❈ ❈

Christmas, my heavenly Father, celebrates Jesus' arrival as a baby—the tender infant who is called the Prince of Peace and the Light of the World. But in order to fully accomplish your purpose on earth, he grew up to become the Suffering Servant, who, through his death and resurrection, opened the way for me to come to you. Your love, Father, is powerful and

profound. It still takes my breath away
to ponder it. Through your Son, the
Savior, you have removed the stain of
my sin and made me your own child.
Praise the Lord!

❄ ❄ ❄

*See what love the Father has given us, that we
should be called children of God; and that is what
we are.... Beloved, we are God's children now; what
we will be has not yet been revealed. What we do
know is this: when he is revealed, we will be like
him, for we will see him as he is.*

—1 John 3:1–2

❄ ❄ ❄

I have learned to trust your love for
me, Lord. That is why I pray. I talk to
you about virtually everything that
comes my way in life. I look to you for

counsel and wisdom, provision and
protection. I would be truly lost if I
could not come to you at all times,
seek your guidance, and cast my cares
on you. Thank you for inviting me
here to this place of communing with
you. Thank you for always having your
doors open and your loving heart
ready to receive me.

※ ※ ※

*"God regards nothing about the prayers of his
children as being too trivial or ordinary,
especially when a bent knee, a bowed head, or
clasped hands accompanies our prayers."*

※ ※ ※

As I consider the goals I'd like to reach
for in the year ahead, loving God,

perhaps the most worthy ones will center around your love—around giving and receiving your love in various ways and in greater measure. If there are things you'd like to see grow and flourish in my life this year, please turn my heart and mind toward what would nurture those things. In all things, God, I pray that I will honor you by loving well and by remaining in your love from moment to moment, day to day, month to month, throughout the year.

❈ ❈ ❈

"When we place ourselves into the care of a loving God, things that we once thought impossible now brim with possibilities. That which had eluded us seems right within our grasp, and we rest in the knowledge that all the guidance and support we need is never more than a prayer away."

❈ ❈ ❈

As the dawn of a new year breaks the horizon, dear Father, I know your eternal love for me goes before me. I ask that you would cause me to live courageously in that love, ready to do and say what is right and good and true in all circumstances. And because I have known your faithful love up to this point in my life, I'm fully confident that all will be well as I move forward and am kept in that same love. Thank you for always walking with me and, at critical times in my life, for carrying me on your loving shoulders. I love you, and I pray in the name of my Lord and Savior, Jesus Christ. Amen.

※ ※ ※

Now may our Lord Jesus Christ himself and God our Father, who loved us and through grace gave us eternal comfort and good hope, comfort your hearts and strengthen them in every good work and word.

—2 Thessalonians 2:16–17

ACKNOWLEDGMENTS

※ ※ ※

Christine A. Dallman is a freelance writer living near Everett, Washington. She is the author of *Daily Devotions for Seniors,* an inspirational resource for maturing adults, as well as coauthor of several other PIL titles.

Marie D. Jones is the author of several best-selling nonfiction books and a contributing author to numerous inspirational books, which include *Echoes of Love: Sisters, Mother, Grandmother, Friends, Graduation, Wedding; A Mother's Daily Prayer Book;* and *When You Lose Someone You Love: A Year of Comfort.* She can be reached at www.mariedjones.com.

PHOTO CREDITS

FRONT COVER: **Photodisc**

American Spirit Images: 227; **Art Explosion:** 63, 180; **Artville:** 136, 247, 326; **Brand X Pictures:** 6, 9, 32, 48, 59, 138, 166, 192, 234, 242, 266, 351, 356, 364, 369; **Corbis:** 289; **Dreamstime:** 133; **Jupiter Images:** 195, 321; **Photodisc:** 24, 37, 82, 92, 100, 103, 108, 118, 123, 126, 131, 145, 153, 158, 162, 165, 170, 201, 207, 212, 217, 220, 239, 250, 259, 263, 270, 274, 279, 284, 294, 302, 309, 319, 333, 334, 339, 344, 361, 373, 381, 383; **Shutterstock:** 9, 29, 45, 53, 66, 71, 74, 79, 87, 97, 148, 175, 185, 190, 196, 231, 255, 299, 314, 353, 376; **Stockbyte:** 41; **Thinkstock:** 13, 14, 19, 115